HOWARD W. HUNTER

Other Books by Francis M. Gibbons

Joseph Smith: Martyr, Prophet of God

Brigham Young: Modern Moses, Prophet of God

John Taylor: Mormon Philosopher, Prophet of God

Wilford Woodruff: Wondrous Worker, Prophet of God

Lorenzo Snow: Spiritual Giant, Prophet of God

Joseph F. Smith: Patriarch and Preacher, Prophet of God

Heber J. Grant: Man of Steel, Prophet of God

George Albert Smith: Kind and Caring Christian, Prophet of God

David O. McKay: Apostle to the World, Prophet of God

Joseph Fielding Smith: Gospel Scholar, Prophet of God

Harold B. Lee: Man of Vision, Prophet of God

Spencer W. Kimball: Resolute Disciple, Prophet of God

Ezra Taft Benson: Statesman, Patriot, Prophet of God

Dynamic Disciples, Prophets of God: Life Stories of the Presidents of The Church of Jesus Christ of Latter-day Saints

HOWARD W. HUNTER

Man of Thought and Independence, Prophet of God

FRANCIS M. GIBBONS

SALT LAKE CITY, UTAH

Visit us at DeseretBook.com

Library of Congress Cataloging-in-Publication Data

Gibbons, Francis M., 1921–

Howard W. Hunter : man of thought and independence, prophet of God / Francis M. Gibbons.

p. cm.

Includes bibliographical references and index.

ISBN 978-1-60641-943-4 (paperbound)

1. Hunter, Howard W., 1907–1995. 2. Church of Jesus Christ of Latter-day Saints—Presidents–Biography. 3. Mormon Church—Presidents—Biography. 4. Mormons—United States—Biography. I. Title.

BX8695.H82G53 2011

289.3092—dc22

[B] 2010040572

Printed in the United States of America

R. R. Donnelley, Harrisonburg, VA

10 9 8 7 6 5 4 3 2 1

To my three friends named John:

John R. Ehlert

John Paul Kennedy

John S. Boyden

Contents

Acknowledgments

I am grateful to Richard Hunter for the encouragement and insights he provided as I undertook to research and write this biography of his noble father. I am also indebted to Eleanor Knowles, who edited some of my earlier writings while employed by Deseret Book, for the detailed research she compiled while writing her biography of President Hunter.

INTRODUCTION

All the Presidents of the restored Church of Jesus Christ of Latter-day Saints have been different from each other in experience, background, occupation, and personality. The winding path to the prophetic office differs in each case. Challenges encountered along the way are never the same. Among the sixteen men who have presided over The Church of Jesus Christ of Latter-day Saints, none presents a more intriguing mosaic of differences than does the subject of this biography: President Howard W. Hunter. Consider, for instance, his occupation before assuming his apostolic-prophetic role: He was a lawyer.

Brigham Young might well have muttered, "You mean a lawyer has entered the prophetic office?" when President Hunter was ordained. Brother Brigham had no use for lawyers. He used some of his most colorful invective in denouncing them. To think of a lawyer in the prophetic chair might, for him, have been beyond reason. To him, the lawyer was the cunning, loquacious, and dishonest shyster who peopled the frontier courts in Ohio, Missouri, and Illinois. They were a bane in the lives of the Latter-day Saints. It is true that now and then the Mormons encountered an honest lawyer, as in the case of General Alexander W. Doniphan, who laid his military career on the line in defense of the Prophet Joseph Smith (see *Comprehensive History of the Church*, 1:490). But lawyers such as he were a rare exception. Brother Brigham and his brethren never encountered a lawyer quite like Howard W. Hunter, an educated, poised, and articulate advocate who reflected in his personal life all the ennobling qualities President Young would have applauded.

Other distinguished lawyers served as counselors in the First Presidency before President Hunter: Presidents J. Reuben Clark Jr., Stephen L Richards, Henry D. Moyle, and Hugh B. Brown. However, President Hunter was the first—and to date the only—lawyer-president of the Church.

Consider also that President Hunter was reared in a part-member home. His mother, Nellie Rasmussen Hunter, was a devoted member of the Church who regularly took Howard with her to meetings in the small branch in Boise, Idaho, where the family lived. His mother also taught Howard to pray and often read the sacred scriptures to him; however, his father, John William Hunter, usually called Will, was not a member of the Church. Will's grandfather John Hunter was converted to the Church in Paisley, Scotland, and migrated to Utah in the early 1860s. Because of misunderstandings and disappointments, John Hunter separated from the Church soon after arriving in Salt Lake City, moving his family first to Montana and then to Wyoming. At the time of John Hunter's disaffection, his son, John, Will's father, was ten years old.

John, Howard's grandfather, never affiliated with the Church. Thus, Howard's father had no direct contact with the Church and, of course, was never baptized. It is inferred that his great-grandfather's disaffection and his grandfather's and father's lack of affiliation with the Church affected Will's attitude toward it. As a result, he was unwilling that his son, Howard, be baptized at the customary age of eight. The depth of Will's resistance is illustrated by the fact that faithful, diligent Nellie pleaded with her husband to relent. He was adamant in his refusal. Given Will Hunter's reputation for intelligence and reasonableness, it must be assumed that his refusal did not represent hatred toward the Church but rather a desire to delay the baptism until Howard was more mature and therefore better able to make a reasoned judgment.

For four years after Howard's eighth birthday, Will's decision had no apparent ill effect upon his son. Howard continued to attend meetings in the branch as before. There he found friendship and support from the branch leaders and the young people. He was just like all the other Mormon boys his age. Then came age twelve, and all his boyhood friends in the branch were ordained deacons. The ordination itself did not affect Howard negatively as he had no idea what it meant. A partial understanding came when all his friends were permitted to pass the sacrament while he sat alone. It was devastating to him. It presented a real crisis in his young life. For the first time he felt different, unaccepted and unwanted among those whom he loved and among whom he had grown up. Very soon Will saw the troubling effect upon Howard of the decision he had made in not approving his son's baptism. And not long thereafter Howard was baptized into the Church. It occurred on April 4, 1920, in the Natatorium, an indoor swimming complex in Boise. He received the Aaronic Priesthood and was ordained a deacon soon after. This inauspicious event, occurring in what was then perceived to be a remote branch of the Church, set Howard W. Hunter on a priesthood path which, seventy-four years later, would lead him to the pinnacle of Church leadership.

Until age twelve, young Howard Hunter had his feet in two worlds: the world of the Church and the world of a nonmember. This dichotomy in his early life created an attitude and a perception which were evident throughout his years. It gave Howard a certain sense of freedom from the strict forms of cultural observance found among other Latter-day Saints raised in a more strict and orthodox environment. Contrast, for instance, Howard's early life and the early life of Gordon B. Hinckley, who succeeded him as President of the Church. President Hinckley's father and a grandfather were both stake presidents. President Hinckley's grandfather, who also was a patriarch, had lived among the Saints in Nauvoo and had pioneered to Utah at the call of the Church. There he had carved out a distinguished life whose whole purpose was to strengthen and expand the interests of the Church. Brother Hinckley's father, Bryant S. Hinckley, a noted Church writer, speaker, and educator, headed a Church school in Salt Lake City and was a confidant of President Heber J. Grant and was President Grant's biographer. Thus the home in which President Hinckley was raised was steeped in Mormon tradition, culture, and doctrine. Family prayers were frequent and fervent, and the Church was the family's main focus.

The contrast with the home in which President Hunter was raised is striking insofar as the Church is concerned. Yet the Hunter home was also one of culture and refinement where love and good feelings flourished and where study and learning were encouraged. While his mother was an important anchor and exemplar for Howard in his faith, his nonmember father set the tone and the direction of the family, as demonstrated by his refusal to allow Howard to be baptized at the age of eight.

As Howard Hunter grew up in the home of his nonmember father, he began to show the characteristics that prompted the title of this biography. In his maturity the qualities of thought and independence shone brightly in his life. They began to glimmer from his boyhood. At age ten he began keeping a thoughtful diary. It was a practice he followed intermittently throughout his life. His early diary opens a window into the thoughts of a young boy who was destined for greatness. He was precise in his entries, often noting such personal habits as the time of rising from his bed. He was loving and kindly in referring to members of his family: his mother, his sister, Dorothy, and his cousins who lived on a farm near Melba, Idaho. He was intrigued by animals on the farm. One of these aroused a poetic response when he wrote: "Woody and I went walking—one lovely summer day—we saw a little rabbit which quickly ran away." He was struck by the sight of a waterfall which fell a hundred feet into a pool where he and Woody went swimming. Afterward they warmed themselves by a fire they made "in a hole in the side of the mountain." Then later, "The water looked so pretty we went swimming again."

The early diary reflects unusual qualities of observation and reporting for a ten-year-old boy, not to mention the discipline it took to record the incidents in a permanent form. It also reflects a quality of thinking about his surroundings and their appearance and of recording their influence upon him.

As President Hunter matured, these qualities became more pronounced and more focused. This perhaps explains in part the special interest he showed in the writings of Napoleon Hill. Mr. Hill wrote a best-selling book titled *Think and Grow Rich*. In it the author extols the power of the human mind. He cites many examples of unusual achievements emanating from its disciplined use. The author also recommends that his readers form groups of so-called "Master Minds," whose purpose is to pool their thoughts in pursuit of worthwhile objectives. Howard formed such a group with several of his associates, which proved to be a rewarding and valuable experience. Such an association was especially meaningful to President Hunter, who believed that we become what we think about. Years after his association with his Master Minds group, Brother Hunter found a small object made by a major corporation on which was etched the single word *Think.* As this coincided so well with his personal philosophy, President Hunter placed this object on his desk. It became, as it were, his motto and a constant reminder of the need to use his mind in analyzing and processing the various challenges he met each day. The author first saw this object in a meeting with Elder Hunter in his office. Later, I recorded this observation in my diary: "It intrigued me that on his desk was a little knickknack with the single word 'Think' on it, thus betraying an independence and individuality not shown by many. Because of his comparative youth, his seniority in the Twelve, and his apparent good health, I may well have spent a pleasant hour today with a future president of the Church" (Author's diary, December 11, 1979).

During the sixteen years I served as the secretary to the First Presidency, I attended hundreds of meetings where President Hunter was in attendance. In the course of these meetings, President Hunter's voice was heard less frequently than almost any other. That is quite amazing when one considers the popular perception of lawyers as being verbose, but it is not to suggest that he sat mute in these meetings. He was always actively involved; however, he did not feel the need to be heard on every subject under discussion. When he did speak, what he said was thoughtful and analytical.

This characteristic is illustrated by the initiative begun during his prophetic administration. As the Lord's prophet, President Hunter asked the members of the Church to always carry a current temple recommend. This he asked even of those who did not live near a temple and who might never use their recommend. Consider the impact of that request, given the criteria one must meet in order to receive a temple recommend: payment of tithing, observance of the Word of Wisdom, honesty, moral cleanliness, and Church activity, among other things. The request suggests a special quality of President Hunter's thinking process. He was aiming at several tangential objectives while focusing on a single one. It is reminiscent of the first and great commandment: to love God with all one's heart, soul, mind, and strength (Mark 12:29–30), and the correlative definition of love: "If ye love me, keep my commandments" (John 14:15).

President Hunter's independent nature was reflected in various ways and in different circumstances. Perhaps a good starting point is his band. At age eighteen he organized a five-piece combo named Hunter's Croonaders, which played for dances throughout the Boise area. Toward the end of 1926, Howard negotiated a contract with the Admiral Oriental Lines to provide music aboard the *SS President Jackson* during a two-month cruise to the Orient. Especially noteworthy is the skill, the confidence, and the independence shown by this eighteen-year-old who had traveled outside Idaho only once to visit relatives in California. Yet he had now undertaken to lead his band to exotic and faraway places. It was a high-wire adventure for a neophyte. But he approached it with independence, poise, and aplomb.

Music played an important role in President Hunter's early life. As the leader of the Croonaders, he was skilled on the piano, drums, and several wind instruments. He enjoyed playing with a group. He enjoyed the camaraderie and the satisfaction of combining his musical talent with those of his friends in providing entertainment for others. The activity had its downside, however. The late hours seriously interfered with his social life. And the atmosphere of the dancing venues did not always meet his standard of propriety. This brought about a deliberate decision to give up his music, which occurred near the time of his marriage to Claire. It was a time of reappraisal as he considered the kind of family life he wanted to create. Given his deepening understanding of the gospel and a growing interest in the law, he brought his musical career to a sudden end. The way he did it had a ritualistic quality about it. He played his last gig with the band, carefully cleaned and wrapped his instruments, and put them away, never to play them again, except on rare family occasions. Many years later he was nearly enticed into assuming the role of piano accompanist for his brethren at their weekly meetings. President Harold B. Lee had played that role for some years and was succeeded by President Spencer W. Kimball. When President Kimball became the President of the Church, he hinted broadly that Elder Hunter should assume the role of accompanist. He adroitly avoided taking the hint. Had the prophet asked him directly to do it, he most assuredly would have done so. As it was, his retirement from musical performance remained intact.

Howard's courting of Claire Jeffs was unique, yes, different. After his and his family's move to Boise, he and Claire belonged to a group of young Latter-day Saints in Los Angeles among whom there was a strong fraternal bond. They enjoyed group activities together: dancing, picnics, movies, and gospel study. There was little steady dating among them, and a date usually consisted of several couples. There came a time, however, when the relationship between Howard and Claire became more focused on each other. They were both employed, Howard at a bank and Claire at a popular department store. In this situation they decided to take their vacations together and settled upon a cruise. They booked passage on a cruise ship, their staterooms on different decks. Their parents were appalled when they learned of the plan. What would people think of two young people, unmarried, taking a cruise together? This young couple wasn't troubled by this objection. They knew who they were and what they were about.

Their independence and self-confidence won over their parents, who set their seal of approval on the cruise. The young couple had a joyous time, dining together in the evening, dancing to the music of the ship's orchestra, and then retiring to their separate staterooms at night. The daylight hours were spent playing shuffleboard or walking the decks, watching the marine life all about them, or just talking about their plans for the future. This was a young couple who did not mortgage today in anticipation of bright tomorrows. They enjoyed life as they lived it, day by day.

The enjoyment of this cruise carried over into their marriage. They decided to drive to Salt Lake City from Los Angeles to be married in the Salt Lake Temple. Knowing Howard as she did, Claire was probably not surprised to see him drive up in a brand-new sports car with red wheels. With the trade-in on his old car and cash he'd saved, Howard owned the new car free and clear.

On returning to California from Utah following their sealing in the Salt Lake Temple, Howard and Claire moved into a luxury apartment near the beach. They remained there for a month, enjoying an upscale lifestyle. Each evening after work, they would take a swim in the ocean before enjoying dinner in their apartment. When the month was over, they moved into a smaller and more affordable place.

The upscaling of their lifestyle with a temporary luxury apartment and a sports car with red wheels should be viewed in light of the circumstances fifty years later. Then-Elder Howard W. Hunter, who could have afforded any automobile of his choice from resources earned during his years as a practicing attorney, drove an automobile ten years old, more or less. It stood out rather conspicuously from the newer, classier models driven by other of the General Authorities. It was but another illustration of a man who was impelled by his own motivations and standards, irrespective of what those around him were doing.

Incidents in the life of President Hunter that further illustrate his independence and individuality are legion. Here are a few:

Elder Hunter was assigned to visit the stake where this author presided, a stake that included two members of the First Presidency among its membership. In preparing for the conference, Elder Hunter asked whether the members of the First Presidency would be present. Being told no, he said with a smile and a chuckle, "Good. We'll do what we want to do!"

Another time, I accompanied Elder Hunter on a stake conference assignment to California. At the Salt Lake airport we took seats awaiting the call to board our plane. We had begun to visit when a woman seated next to Elder Hunter said in a sharp tone, "You are in my husband's seat." Caught by surprise, Elder Hunter paused as if processing what the woman had said and then with a smile and in a gentle voice said, "Oh, I don't see him here." His kindly manner having disarmed the woman's hostility, we moved to other seats.

Later in life, Elder Hunter underwent major surgery on his back, which resulted in his inability to walk. A special chair was built that enabled him to speak during general conference while seated. He was determined to discontinue speaking while in a chair. Through great effort and with assistance from a therapist, he was able to move about and to stand. Later at a general conference session when he was called on to speak, he stood and carefully moved to the pulpit. During the address, he lost his balance and fell backward. Immediately members of the Twelve sprang to help, lifting him up in place behind the pulpit. With no explanation or comment, Elder Hunter completed his sermon, seemingly without missing a word.

This example of stoic independence was likewise illustrated at a talk he delivered at a devotional in the Brigham Young University Marriott Center. During his address, a man walked to the pulpit carrying a small box. He told Elder Hunter the box contained an explosive device, which he threatened to detonate unless Elder Hunter read a statement he thrust before him. Elder Hunter calmly refused. After ten minutes of confusion and suspense, the man was subdued and removed from the stand. Again, without explanation or comment, Elder Hunter continued with his address, reading the phrase, "Life has a fair number of challenges," and adding, "as demonstrated."

For a few years before her death in October 1983, Sister Claire Hunter suffered several serious illnesses. At length she was placed in a care center. Elder Hunter visited her every day, talking to her quietly, expressing his love, and telling her about his daily activities and those of the family. It was a sad day for Elder Hunter when his sweetheart passed away. They had been happily married for more than fifty years. She was the love of his life and the mother of their children. For seven years after her death, Elder Hunter lived alone. They were difficult years, not only because of Claire's absence but because of serious physical difficulties he suffered.

President Hunter's single status ended suddenly and dramatically on April 10, 1990. On that day, without explanation or preamble, he announced at the end of a meeting with the Quorum of the Twelve, "I'm going to be married this afternoon." He said his bride was Inis Stanton, a member of the Church he had known in California many years before, who was then serving as a receptionist in the Church Office Building. He said the ceremony would be performed by President Gordon B. Hinckley that afternoon in a sealing room in the temple with President Thomas S. Monson and Sister Stanton's bishop acting as witnesses. No one else would be present. The feeling of shock in the room was palpable. Indeed, one of those present said his jaw dropped to the floor when he heard the announcement. Only Elder James E. Faust of the Twelve knew in advance of the marriage, he having made arrangements to have the marriage license issued without publicity. The careful, precise way this significant event was handled attests to President Hunter's skill and his independent character. Once he and Sister Stanton had made the decision to marry, only those who had to know were brought into the picture. This maintained their privacy and avoided needless publicity. Afterward the details of their courting were made known to their associates and family members.

President Hunter's individuality was also shown in his method of teaching. He believed history could be taught best by visiting sites where important historical events had occurred. For his own education, he made it a practice whenever he was in the area to visit the homes of early Church leaders, thereby providing context for later study. Two instances illustrate his style in teaching others through gatherings at historic sites:

While in Israel during one of his many visits there, he joined with David Galbraith to lead a group of Brigham Young University students on a trek up Mount Sinai. Before the trek, there were discussions about the significance of the mount and the extraordinary events that occurred there when Moses received the tablets of the law. At the base of the mount, Elder Hunter and other older members of the group mounted camels while the younger, more vigorous members hiked up. At a point in the climb when it became too steep and rugged for the camels, Elder Hunter and others dismounted and climbed within sight of the summit. It was cold with heavy winds. Because the summit was near and clearly in view, it was decided not to climb further. Elder Hunter observed, with his usual good humor, that he couldn't imagine Moses had climbed any higher.

The experience of the young students of hiking Mount Sinai with an Apostle of the Lord will remain with them throughout their lives. Doubtless many of them recorded the incident in their journals with comments about the impact of the experience upon them. By this means, the effect of President Hunter's teaching will have an influence which will extend into generations yet unborn.

In October 1963, Elder Hunter held a seminar for mission presidents serving in the American Midwest. They gathered first in Nauvoo, Illinois, together with their wives. Taking advantage of the locale, which bristles with Mormon history, Elder Hunter sought to teach the participants an unforgettable lesson. He arranged for the wives to stay overnight in the Nauvoo home of President John Taylor. He then led the mission presidents to nearby Carthage, Illinois, where arrangements had been made for them to stay overnight in the jail where the Prophet Joseph Smith and his brother Hyrum were martyred. Gathering in the room where the killings took place, with the blood of the martyrs still evident on the floor, Elder Hunter invited M. Ross Richards—a grandson of Willard Richards, who was with Joseph and Hyrum when they were murdered—to relate the circumstances of that infamous day. Then the brethren sang all of the verses of "A Poor Wayfaring Man of Grief" (*Hymns*, no. 29). After sharing their testimonies and evening prayers, the brethren bedded down in rooms on the second floor of the jail. It was typical of President Hunter's leadership style that he called on a mission president to relate the story of what happened at the time of the killings. Like the Prophet Joseph Smith, Elder Hunter never felt the need to play the leading role in every Church gathering he directed.

CHAPTER ONE

The Awakening—Tracing Ancestral Roots

Howard W. Hunter knew little about his ancestry during his early life. His great-grandfather John Hunter seems to have brought little if any family information or records with him when he emigrated from Scotland in the early 1860s. John Hunter's disaffection from the Church and his life in remote areas of the western United States severed him from the Church and its library facilities from which he might have learned something about his ancestry. John Hunter Jr. and Will Hunter suffered the same disability. As with other principles of the gospel, once Howard Hunter became aware of the importance of gathering family genealogical information and family stories, he became absorbed in the process. He was avid in gathering names, dates, and places and connecting family lines as a means of facilitating vicarious temple work. His later roles as Church Historian and as president of the Genealogical Society added important emphasis to these endeavors.

Over the years, as Elder Hunter fulfilled his apostolic responsibilities by traveling over the earth, he made it a point to visit the towns and villages where his ancestors had lived. By this means he gave context to his genealogical records, putting a face, as it were, to the written page. Thus in 1972 while in Europe, he and Sister Hunter, accompanied by mission president Paul L. Pehrson and his wife, visited places where his Danish ancestors had lived. They took pictures, visited parish churches, and interviewed persons at the various sites. At one village in Denmark, Elder Hunter found the ancient church where his great-grandfather Morten Rasmussen was christened and members of his family had worshipped. During this tour, Elder Hunter visited every site in Denmark which he was aware of where his Danish ancestors had lived and worshipped. It sparked in him deep feelings of love and appreciation for this heritage, bequeathed to him through his beloved mother, Nellie Rasmussen. While traveling in Norway on another occasion, he visited Norwegian villages once inhabited by members of the family of his great-grandmother, Nilla Pedersen. (Her name is cited in some other sources as Torgersen, her father's surname, though the Norwegian—and Danish—naming system gave a child the father's first name plus "sen" or "son" as their surname. Thus, Nilla Pedersen was the child of Peder Torgersen, who was the child of Torger Pedersen, etc. When they came to America, the authorities would have required Nilla to take her father's surname as hers, thus creating the confusion among sources.)

President Hunter's Scottish ancestry came into dramatic focus on October 20, 1987. On that day he was honored at an early birthday luncheon (see "News of the Church," *Ensign*, January 1988,

75). It was hosted by Elder David B. Haight of the Twelve, a former president of the Scottish Mission. Also attending was Elder Bernard P. Brockbank, the first president of the then–Scottish-Irish mission. Present too was Mr. Charles Hunter, heir of the Scottish clan Hunter, who was destined to become the World Chief of the clan and the thirtieth Laird of Hunterston, the clan's ancestral home. President Hunter was given a framed certificate, recognizing him as a lifetime member of the Clan Hunter and lauding "his great example of humanitarian service and love for all mankind" and acknowledging him as "one of the noblest scions of a noble race, and one of the greatest Hunters of them all." President Hunter also was presented with a tartan and a framed silkscreen print of a painting of Hunterston Castle, located on the west coast of Scotland. While President Hunter's innate modesty constrained him to downplay the generous compliments in the certificate, he appreciated the sentiment and observed that while he had never lived in Scotland, "many of us feel it is our homeland."

This event and what it revealed greatly expanded the landscape of President Hunter's ancestry and opened up broad avenues of new family research. The Hunters of Scotland trace their ancestry to the Normans who immigrated to Great Britain following the conquest of England in 1066 by William of Normandy. Their loyalty to the Norman court resulted in a regal gift to the family of a thousand acres in western Scotland which became known as Hunters Toune. On May 2, 1374, Scotland's king Robert II confirmed this royal charter to William Hunter, the laird of Hunterston Castle. For more than six hundred years before Charles Hunter's meeting with President Hunter, successive lairds had presided over Hunterston Castle. The thought of such longevity must have been enormous to one born and raised in Boise, Idaho, where cultural age was computed in decades, not centuries.

President Hunter toured Hunterston Castle in September 1989 with his son Richard. While there, he obtained a brief history of the castle which, upon his return to Salt Lake City, was copied into his personal record. While in Scotland on this occasion, President Hunter and Richard also visited Paisley Abbey, founded in 1163, which is thought to be the place where John Hunter, President Hunter's great-grandfather, was baptized a member of the Church of Scotland.

CHAPTER TWO

THE BOISE YEARS—FAMILY TIES

The city of Boise, Idaho, in the western part of the state, was founded in the early 1860s when gold was discovered in the area. Like a magnet, the thought of gold brought to the area a flood of miners who were seeking instant wealth and the luxuries money can buy. With the miners came the usual cast of characters which accompanied the development of any mining town: the suppliers, the merchants, the lawyers, the hostelers, the saloonkeepers, the gamblers, and the prostitutes. The subsequent orderly and sedate development of the community which became the capital of the state never completely eradicated the raucous flavor of its beginnings.

This, then, was the community into which Howard W. Hunter was born on November 14, 1907, less than fifty years after the gold rush which gave it birth. The later development of Boise had brought with it the usual complement of churches—Catholic,

Protestant, and a small branch of The Church of Jesus Christ of Latter-day Saints. At the time of Howard's birth, the Latter-day Saints constituted a tiny percentage of the city's population. This was unlike the towns in the eastern part of the state, Idaho Falls, Rexburg, Sugar City, Rigby, and others where the Latter-day Saint population was predominant. In Boise, not only were there few members of the Church but these members were largely looked down upon and denigrated. This attitude seems to have derived in large part from negative perceptions of the Church driven by the practice of plural marriage, which was discontinued only seventeen years before Howard's birth. These negative perceptions continued through the years, even until May 1984, when the Boise Temple was dedicated. As the temple neared completion, there were angry demonstrations in the streets of Boise, denouncing the Church and railing against the temple. Apparently frustrated that their verbal attacks were ineffective, some of those opposed resorted to physical assault, spraying graffiti on the walls and detonating an explosive device near the temple which shattered windows. It was necessary to sandblast the walls to remove the graffiti before the temple could be dedicated.

During his youth in Boise, Howard seemed oblivious to the contentious issues facing the Church. There were too many interesting things for a young boy to do which took precedence over anything else. His parents encouraged scholarship. The encyclopedia and other good books found in the home were read with the children, as were books borrowed from the public library. A piano which the children learned to play encouraged musical interests and introduced a cultural quality into their home. Howard later learned to play several instruments which led him to a temporary career in music.

Over the years, Howard presided over a menagerie of pets (dogs, cats, and rabbits); collected bird eggs, stamps, and coins; worked in the family garden and orchard; held a variety of jobs, among which were selling newspapers and working as a "cash boy" at a department store; and began to keep a diary. He also became absorbed in Scouting, receiving the second Eagle Scout award given in Boise. We gain insight into the competitive fire that burned within this young man from a statement he made about the boy who was Boise's first Eagle Scout: "The race was on between Edwin Phipps of Troop 6 and me," wrote Howard, referring to the scramble for merit badges, prerequisites for the Eagle award. Howard's competitiveness was always accompanied by genuine friendliness and goodwill. He never seemed to be competing. He was always gracious and kind, the sort of young man who tipped his hat to adults on the sidewalk and who, like a good Scout, surrendered his seat on the streetcar to the elderly.

In high school, academics had to compete for Howard's attention with the ROTC, music, and afterschool employment. In the ROTC, he was eventually commissioned a major, the highest rank at his level. In addition to the piano, he learned to play the marimba, drums, saxophone, clarinet, trumpet, and violin. He worked alternately as a golf caddie, in a pharmacy, an art store, and a hotel.

After Howard's graduation from high school in June 1926, the success of the Croonaders playing for dances around Boise led to a contract to provide dance and concert music and accompaniment for silent movies aboard the *SS President Jackson* during a two-month luxury cruise to the Orient. Embarking from Seattle, Washington, on January 8, 1927, the five-man combo played not only aboard ship but also in several hotels at stops along the way. At ports of call in Yokohama and Kobe, Japan; Shanghai and Hong

Kong, China; and Manila, the Philippines, the young Americans were exposed to foreign cultures and economies as they toured these ancient exotic cities. While at Yokohama, Howard and two companions traveled to Tokyo where, by chance, they saw the body of the deceased emperor, Yoshihito, lying in state at a Buddhist temple near the royal palace. They also saw the emperor's oldest son, Hirohito, who succeeded him. There was unrest in Shanghai caused by conflicts between communist and nationalist forces outside the city. Within a few years, during World War II, the names of Hirohito and Generalissimo Chiang Kai-shek (commander of the nationalist forces) would become household names throughout the United States.

Following his return from the Orient, Howard tried his hand at several things: selling shoes at Falks Department Store, working with a partner to open a supper club called the Plantation Roadhouse, and engaging in an advertising promotion that involved posting attractive placards featuring local businesses and containing announcements and time schedules. Because none of these ventures held the prospect of a permanent career path, Howard, while mulling over his options, traveled to Los Angeles, California, in March 1928 for a short vacation.

• • •

A joyful surprise awaited Howard on his return from the Oriental cruise on March 11, 1927. His father had been baptized a member of the Church the previous month. The word *surprise* may be misplaced, as the family and everyone in the Boise ward had the sense this would happen. Will acted like a Latter-day Saint. He was an exemplary husband and father. Employed by the Boise

Interurban Railroad as a motorman for many years, he had built the family home on a quarter-acre lot in a new subdivision west of the Boise city limits. Will had two assistants in the construction: the brother-in-law of Nellie's aunt Christie Moore and two-year-old Howard. The reader must not discount the idea of this toddler helping in the construction, because Howard's father had purchased a little hammer for him which he used diligently in pounding nails into the flooring. The incident suggests the genuine love Will Hunter had for his son.

Once the new home was completed, Will planted fruit trees and a garden, which Howard helped to tend. Will was always intensely interested in the education of his children. There was a family library which included a good encyclopedia and a piano, which both children learned to play. Eleven-year-old Howard recorded the excitement attending the arrival of the piano: "Nov. 1. Today is sister's birthday. Mother and Dad gave her a thimble a little doll and a pair of slippers. I gave her a little Kewpie doll. John Henry moved in next door. All the kids were over there watching them unload when a big dray came in. All us kids went to see what it was. It was a player piano for sister's birthday, but it was really for both of us."

As Howard became involved in Scouting and the ROTC, Will was a supporter and cheerleader, providing constant encouragement. As Howard's career unfolded, his father's love and admiration for him was unbounded. The son's distinction as an attorney and his prominence as a Church leader in Southern California were recognitions unmatched by anyone in the Hunter family. This seems to have been a source of amazement to Will Hunter. What had impelled this young man to break out of the mold of family patterns and traditions to achieve so significantly? A canvass of the Hunter ancestral line, extending from President Hunter back to Scotland, reveals no one with the qualities of mind and character and the persistence which he displayed. He seemed to be marching to the cadence of a far distant drum. Can it be that Howard Hunter was impelled by hints and spiritual nudges from long ago, from his premortal associations with the Almighty and with those destined to play leading roles in the drama of earth life? Whatever the cause or the source of it, there were clear spiritual overtones in the life of Howard Hunter.

As Will and Nellie Hunter watched their son become a successful bishop and then a stake president, their expectations for his future increased as did their desire to show themselves fully supportive of him and his work. It was then they decided to surprise him. Without Howard's knowledge, they prepared themselves to receive temple recommends which would entitle them to be sealed in the temple as man and wife for eternity and to have Howard sealed to them in an eternal relationship. They decided to spring their surprise at a session in the Mesa Temple to which members of Howard's stake had traveled. (This was before the Los Angeles Temple had been dedicated.) President Hunter recorded the significant event: "While I was speaking to the congregation, my father and mother came into the chapel dressed in white. I had no idea my father was prepared for his temple blessings, although Mother had been anxious about it for some time. I was so overcome with emotion that I was unable to continue to speak. President Pearce [the temple president] came to my side and explained the reason for the interruption. When my father and mother came to the temple that morning they asked the president not to mention to me that they were there because they wanted it to be a birthday surprise. This was a birthday I have never forgotten because that day they were endowed and I had the privilege of witnessing their sealing, following which I was sealed to them." On April 30, 1956, after the Los Angeles Temple was dedicated, Howard's sister, Dorothy Hunter Rasmussen, was sealed to her parents.

The two Hunter children were raised in comfortable, secure circumstances. Their father's employment as a motorman in Boise's transit system provided adequate, regular income. The family home in a new development featured modern furnishings and equipment. Encouragement from their parents promoted scholarship, musical training, and good social skills. The Hunter children had a host of friends both within and outside the Mormon community. They enjoyed family outings in the Hupmobile, the automobile which served the family for several years. The Hupmobile's untimely demise occurred when Dorothy crashed it into the closed doors of the garage. She had persuaded her mother to let her drive the car without divulging that she knew how to start and drive the car but had no clue about stopping it. After the trauma of losing the Hupmobile had subsided, Will purchased a new Overland Whippet sedan which was, Howard said, "our pride and joy."

Dorothy had certain fiery qualities which Howard did not possess. This characteristic shone brightly in a confrontation with several boys who were older than Howard. These boys were of the character which drew courage from their superior age, size, and numbers. They had stolen Howard's cap and had thrown it on the trolley tracks. When they did it again, Nellie was agitated to say the least. Picking up on her mother's anger, Dorothy the avenger sprang into action, seeking out the gang of boys and confronting them: "If you don't lay off, I'll beat you up." Lacking the physical capacity to vindicate her threat, the young girl's chutzpah and menace apparently carried the day, for we hear no more about the gang and its mischief.

The incident reflects the deep love Dorothy had for her brother and the pride she had in him. She seemed to sense instinctively that he was someone special. It was pleasing to her to see that all her girl friends were attracted to Howard, who was growing into a handsome young man.

In later life, Dorothy was a great comfort and benefactor to her brother. During periods when both Howard and Claire were experiencing serious physical problems, Dorothy was there to take care of Claire, which gave Howard some respite in the face of his own challenges. Also, when Claire was well enough to do so, Dorothy would accompany her to general conference sessions; but instead of sitting in the seat reserved for her among the wives of the General Authorities, Claire would sit in the front of the tabernacle with Dorothy in an area reserved for visiting dignitaries. During periods when Claire was unable to travel, and after her passing, Dorothy occasionally accompanied President Hunter on his overseas assignments. These occasions invariably reminded them of their early years in Boise in the home of their parents.

Family memories also included grandparents and great-grandparents. Their grandparents John and Josephine Nowell Hunter, who were Will's parents, lived in Boise until Howard was ten years old. He and Dorothy visited them often. Grandpa Hunter was a soft touch, usually giving the grandchildren money with which to purchase their favorite confections at a nearby store. In the grandchildren's minds, their grandparents were celebrities because they lived next door to U.S. Senator William Borah. Grandpa Hunter enjoyed talking politics with the senator, who ingratiated himself with the neighborhood children by playing softball with them on occasion. Howard and Dorothy also remembered visiting with great-grandfather Anders Christensen at his home in Mount

Pleasant, Utah. Nellie had taken them there on the train to visit her relatives. Howard vividly remembered his aged ancestor, who spent most of the time in a chair from which he caught Howard with the crook of his cane each time he walked by. Anders Christensen, born in Denmark, had married Nilla Pedersen, a native of Norway. Nilla had passed away by the time of their visit but, as noted previously, Howard visited her birthplace years later during an apostolic tour.

These family ties were important to Howard and Dorothy. When they lived with their parents in Los Angeles, they became better acquainted with members of the Nowell family, to whom they were related through Howard's grandmother Josephine Hunter.

CHAPTER THREE

Growing in a New Place

When Howard returned from his Oriental cruise, he was nineteen years old and uncertain about his next move. He had made no definite plans for the future. For a year he engaged in a series of ventures already mentioned, including selling shoes, pursuing an advertising placards promotion, and toying with the idea of a supper club. None of these held out the prospect of a lifetime career. By the spring of 1928, he was at a crossroad and felt the need for a change of scene in order to appraise his situation and to sort out his options for the future. This decision was triggered by a downturn in his advertising campaign while working in Pocatello, Idaho. Acting upon a previously received invitation from Bill Salisbury, one of the Croonaders, to visit him in California, Howard checked out of his hotel in Pocatello on March 8, 1928, and headed for California.

Anxious for a little adventure, he decided to hitchhike. This was not an unusual thing for a young man to do at that time and place. He was on the road for five days. He spent his nights in hotels along the way, except at Meadow, Utah. There he found that the local "hotel" was a private residence with two rooms for rent, both of which were occupied. In this situation, Howard had to improvise. "A school bus was parked in front of the school and it was unlocked. I lay down in the long seat, pulled the leather jacket of the driver over me and spent the night." The driver was hardly pleased to find Howard in his bus early the next morning and brusquely ordered him off. It is a reasonable assumption that a school bus driver in Meadow, Utah, at that time was a Latter-day Saint. If indeed he was a member of the Church, one could compose an interesting tale about the shelterless prophet and the irate Mormon bus driver.

Howard arrived in Upland, California, Bill Salisbury's home, on March 13, 1928. Here he was in the Golden State, the land of promise, whose mild climate, inviting beaches, abundant citrus groves, and vibrant economy had attracted tens of thousands of newcomers who were seeking a better and an easier life. The development of the movie industry and the celebrity and the wealth of its star performers added a glitter and sheen to the city which reflected an aura of glamour and excitement. At the time, California was in an upward spiral of unusual prosperity. Jobs were plentiful. Unemployment was practically nil. Opportunity was all around for anyone with intelligence, energy, imagination, and perseverance. It seemed to be a place tailor-made for twenty-year-old Howard Hunter.

It is hard to believe that the booming economy Howard found in Southern California in March 1928 was only nineteen months away from Black Tuesday—October 29, 1929, the day of the market crash which heralded the beginning of the Great Depression. No one knew what was coming, except perhaps a clairvoyant few who correctly foresaw the economic disaster which lay ahead. Howard did not foresee it, nor did his friend Bill Salisbury. They spent nine pleasant days together. Bill's occasional employment prevented him from spending all the time with Howard, who used the interval to become acquainted with his new surroundings. Three days after arriving, he purchased a Model T Ford for five dollars. It was a topless two-seater, "just the thing to take us around." With no responsibilities other than to care for himself, Howard spent a carefree month tooling around Los Angeles in his car. He spent a lot of time on the beaches that abound in Southern California, once sleeping overnight on Venice Beach. He and Bill Salisbury found another Croonader, the saxophone player, with whom they shared pleasant memories of their Oriental tour. Howard looked up his father's uncle Edward Nowell who lived with his wife, Lyde, and their children in nearby Huntington Beach. At the Nowell's invitation, Howard moved in with them, enjoying their hospitality and swimming at the beach with his cousins. He became a member of the Huntington Beach Ward, whose chapel was within easy walking distance from the Nowell home. In a gesture of friendship and gratitude for inviting him into the Nowell home, Howard accompanied his Aunt Lyde to the Wednesday evening prayer meetings of her Protestant church on several occasions. Meanwhile, he was acquiring a new set of friends and progressing in his understanding of LDS doctrine by activity in the Huntington Beach Ward.

Howard's inaugural month in California was not devoted entirely to social and Church activities. He spent several days working at the Sunkist packing plant. One day was spent unloading and stacking bundles of wood used to make fruit crates. Then he spent a day loading boxed oranges into a refrigerated railway car. And finally, he spent a day sorting lemons from a conveyor belt. This was especially difficult, as Howard's color blindness made it almost impossible to grade the lemons according to their color at the tip.

When Howard first arrived in California, his plan had been to remain only a few days. After he had observed and tasted the vibrant lifestyle found there, he decided to remain permanently. That decision made, the first item on his agenda was to find employment. His experience at Sunkist turned him away from work as a stevedore or other physical labor. The manner in which he found two jobs one month after arriving in California attests to both his initiative and to the health of the local job market. On April 7, while purchasing a pair of shoes in Huntington Beach, he mentioned to the clerk he had sold similar shoes in Boise. Out of the conversation which followed, he was hired to sell shoes in that store on Saturdays. Deciding he wanted to be a banker, he went to the Bank of Italy on April 23 to apply for a job. He was hired on the spot. The following day he went to work at the bank's main office in downtown Los Angeles, where he learned how to use the bank's machines which calculated deposits and withdrawals. Imbued with the need to increase his education, that evening he enrolled for adult education at Huntington Beach High School.

At the Bank of Italy, Howard met Alma Nelson "Ned" Redding, a Latter-day Saint who had recently returned from the North Central States Mission. They became fast friends, both enrolling for evening classes at the American Institute of Banking. This entailed Howard's withdrawal from evening classes at the high school.

Howard's acquaintance with Ned Redding and his membership in the Huntington Beach Ward led him into association with a group of young Latter-day Saints in the area. Their social activities revolved around the Church. MIA-sponsored dances and theatricals were favorites of the young people. They also enjoyed attending sacrament and other Church services in different wards. They would attend in groups, which turned their attendance into both a worship service and a social affair. It was not uncommon for them to attend Church services in more than one ward in a single day. The effect of this was to create an unusual camaraderie among all the young people in the area, regardless of ward or stake affiliation. Howard entered into these activities with great enthusiasm. It was quite a revelation to him, given the small Latter-day Saint population among which he had been raised. Yet because of his experiences with the Croonaders, he was more accustomed to the aura of the ballroom than were any of his new friends in California.

In early June 1928, only a few weeks after arriving in Los Angeles, Howard attended an MIA-sponsored M Men and Gleaners dance in the Wilshire Ward. It proved to be the most significant dance Howard would attend during his lifetime. It was a date affair, and his friend Ned Redding's date was Clara May "Claire" Jeffs. Following the dance, the group went to the beach. During the course of the evening, Howard became acquainted with Claire Jeffs for the first time. There seemed to be a natural affinity between them. As a result, the next time he and Ned Redding double-dated, Howard "took Claire, and Ned went with someone else." From the time of the MIA dance on June 8, 1928, the relationship between Howard and Claire flowered, resulting ultimately in their marriage and more than fifty years of happy and successful wedded life.

A full-time job at the bank, a Saturday morning job selling shoes, evening classes at the American Institute of Banking, MIA dances and theatricals, and regular, sometimes heroic, attendance at sacrament meetings would appear to be a full plate of activity for anyone. Not so for twenty-year-old Howard Hunter. In the midst of such a swirl, he and his friend Ned Redding joined the Los Angeles Thrift Chorus. This group derived its name from its method of financing through member contributions. The chorus performed in church venues throughout the area and had performed at the dedication of the Mesa Temple the previous year. At the time Howard and Ned joined the chorus, it was preparing for a summer performance at the Hollywood Bowl. They rehearsed Thursday evenings at the Adams Ward. Because the Institute of Banking classes were to finish later in the summer, Howard saw the opportunity to fill that void by restarting his dance band career. After the family shipped his instruments from Boise, Howard caught on as a drummer with a local combo. This activity would continue intermittently until shortly before his marriage to Claire.

The glowing reports Howard made to his family about the excitement and glamour of life in California prompted them to leave Boise and join him in Los Angeles. The timing was perfect for Will, as major changes were afoot in the Boise Transit System for which he had worked for twenty years. When Howard returned from work to his uncle Edward Nowell's home on September 4, 1928, he found his parents and Dorothy there, having just arrived from Boise.

It was a joyous time for Howard to be reunited with his family. After spending a few days with the Nowells, Will and Nellie and their children moved into an apartment within the boundaries of the Adams Ward. Soon after, the membership records of the family were transferred into that ward and there then began a process of remarkable spiritual growth in the life of Howard W. Hunter.

It seems that from his earliest youth, Howard had an innate knowledge and testimony of the gospel and of the reality of God and His Son, Jesus Christ. This is suggested by the exemplary life he had lived and the quality of his character. It appears also from the impulsive twenty-five-dollar commitment he made toward the construction of the chapel in Boise, although at the time he could scarcely afford it. At the same time it seems clear that when Howard arrived in California, his understanding of the gospel was sketchy at best. This can be accounted for by his upbringing in a part-member home and by minimal gospel scholarship among the members in the remote Boise Branch. In Howard's growing-up years there was no correlation program which makes it possible now for an active Latter-day Saint to be taught the gospel in its fulness several times during one's lifetime.

In California, for the first time in his life—and especially after becoming a member of the Adams Ward—this future prophet became aware of the full scope and meaning of the gospel. "Although I had attended Church classes most of my life," Howard wrote, "my first real awakening to the gospel came in a Sunday School class in Adams Ward taught by Brother Peter A. Clayton. He had a wealth of knowledge and the ability to inspire young people. I studied the lessons, read the outside assignments he gave us and participated in speaking on assigned subjects. I suddenly became aware of the real meaning of some of the gospel principles, an understanding of the degrees of glory and the requirements of celestial expectation. As Brother Clayton taught and instructed us, I think of this period of my life as the time the truths of the gospel commenced to unfold. I always had a testimony of the gospel, but suddenly I commenced to understand."

This infusion of knowledge was like drink to a thirsty man. He could never get enough of it. And when newly acquired knowledge of the gospel suggested the need for some action to be taken by him, he responded promptly. So when Howard learned from Brother Clayton about the purpose and significance of a patriarchal blessing,

he acted immediately. "That day I went to see Brother Ge
Wride, the stake patriarch, and he asked me to come to t
fice in the mission home behind the Adams Ward chapel the next Sunday." After visiting briefly, the patriarch gave Howard a blessing which would be a guide and an inspiration to him throughout his life. Among other significant things, the patriarch told him that he had exhibited "strong leadership among the hosts of heaven" and had been ordained "to perform an important work in mortality in bringing to pass purposes with relation to His chosen people."

This process of learning and understanding the principles of the gospel for the first time continued with Howard through the years. For instance, he first learned and understood the principle of paying a full tithe when he went to his bishop for a temple recommend as he and Claire prepared to travel to Salt Lake City to be sealed in the temple. As he discussed these plans, the bishop expressed doubt whether Howard could afford to assume the responsibilities of married life. It soon became apparent the bishop's doubts were based upon a calculation of Howard's income in light of the amount of his tithing donations. As the conversation proceeded, he became aware that tithing meant a tenth of his total income, an amount far greater than he had been contributing. This realization also brought the sinking feeling he might not be qualified to receive a temple recommend, thwarting his marriage plans. When the understanding bishop was made aware of Howard's rearing in a part-member home in the remote Boise Branch, he overlooked Howard's mistake on the condition that he be a full tithe payer in the future. In discussing this embarrassing situation with Claire, he found she had always paid a full tithing. They agreed that as a married couple, they would always pay a full tithe, an agreement they kept with gratitude and fullness of heart.

This incident and others which reflect Howard's imperfect understanding of the principles of the gospel as he grew up gave him special empathy for members of the Church whose conduct did not quite measure up to the standards of a Latter-day Saint. He was forgiving and understanding of members struggling with issues of disobedience and actual or perceived shortcomings. Latter-day Saints of this kind would always find an ally and supporter in Howard Hunter. This attitude crossed over into his activity in the apostolic councils. In his reports to these councils he would never mention the names of local leaders whose conduct or attitude were out of line. He would resolve these issues on the ground but would not air them with his brethren unless the matter was of major importance. This avoided the possibility of someone's reputation being needlessly tarnished.

While Howard grew spiritually in his understanding of the gospel during the first years in California, it was still a time of joyful exuberance for him. He reveled in the social scene. He enjoyed benign partying with his friends, at the beach or on the dance floor or on the stage. At one MIA theatrical he amused his friends by appearing on the stage in female drag.

The 1928 presidential election was a crucial one, although most people—Howard included—took it lightly. The country was still in an optimistic mood. The economy was booming, jobs were plentiful, and the future looked rosy. The presidential election pitted Herbert Hoover, a Republican bureaucrat, against Al Smith, a popular Catholic politician. Howard and his friends Ned Redding and John Madsen decided to have a little fun ridiculing this election which they considered to be a joke. They decided to go for drama. They went to the intersection of Seventh Street and Broadway in downtown Los Angeles. There they set up fruit boxes on which they stood and began to debate the political issues of the day. Howard pretended to be Al Smith, Ned was Herbert Hoover, and John Madsen stood in for the mayor of Los Angeles.

The boys had great fun bantering back and forth as they discoursed on the current political issues. The spectacle of these three handsome young men orating in the middle of the intersection drew large crowds on the adjacent sidewalks. Meanwhile, automobile traffic was heavily impeded by the presence of the three speakers in the intersection. The traffic jam soon drew the attention of the police, who broke up the rally. Howard noted with a sense of satisfaction, "We got away." The incident reveals fun-loving innocent youths expressing their frustration in an unorthodox way. The novelty of it tends to obscure the depth of their knowledge of current events and the level of their oratorical ability. One who can stand in a busy intersection of a major city and intelligently debate political issues is at once intelligent, articulate, and courageous, qualities possessed by Howard Hunter in abundance.

CHAPTER FOUR

A Wife and a New Life

Mention has been made already about Howard abruptly closing out his musical career as he prepared for marriage. Several things combined to bring about this change. His increased knowledge of the gospel and his patriarchal blessing had placed his life in a grand, eternal context he had not understood before. He now realized he was a literal, spiritual offspring of the Almighty God and, therefore, had within him the potential for godhood, which could come to fruition depending upon his obedience and diligence.

Brother Peter Clayton's teaching about the three degrees of glory also had made Howard aware of the importance and significance of celestial marriage. Given the alacrity with which Howard had responded to new principles taught him, as in the instances of patriarchal blessings and tithing, it must be assumed that marriage to the right person in the right place was very much on his mind during his years of socializing in California. While Claire Jeffs had impressed him at that memorable dance in June 1928, she clearly had not come into focus at that time as the one he would marry. During the three years which followed, Howard often dated Claire as well as other girls among the large group of Latter-day Saint youth in the Los Angeles area.

Howard was especially attracted to Claire from the beginning. There was a genuine quality in her demeanor and a certain elegance. At the time of their first meeting, Claire was employed by Blackstones, an upscale department store which catered to the Hollywood set and other women of wealth. Claire had modeled there and at the time was the assistant personnel manager. That she had done so well was a tribute to her intelligence and industry. As a high school student in Salt Lake City where she was born, Claire had worked for the Mountain States Telephone Company.

She moved to Los Angeles in 1926 with her parents, Jacob and Martha Jeffs, two years before Howard arrived. Her father was a successful builder in Salt Lake City and had moved to California, enticed by glowing reports of the booming California economy. In Los Angeles, Jacob Jeffs built a large, comfortable family home in which Claire found love and security. The Church was her spiritual and social haven. Like Howard, Claire had been raised in a part-member home, her father not being a member of the Church. Her mother, Martha, was a devoted member who was always active, serving successively as an officer in the auxiliary organizations, as a teacher, and as a temple worker. It was from her mother that Claire acquired a deep grounding in the Church and an understanding of its doctrines. Martha's mother, Maria Emilie Reckzeh, was baptized into the Church in West Prussia near the village of Grabig. Maria Emilie's father, a staunch Lutheran, promptly evicted her and her two daughters from the family home. They were forever shunned by their family. In time, Maria Emilie immigrated to Utah with her two daughters, where she was active in the Church until her death. When Howard and Claire were married in June 1931, her grandmother Maria Emilie was with them in the Salt Lake Temple.

Howard and Claire's temple sealing was performed by Elder Richard R. Lyman of the Twelve. He counseled them to avoid debt and to never live beyond their means. It was good counsel for a young couple beginning their married life twenty months after the stock market had crashed on "Black Tuesday," October 29, 1929. The effects of that crash were not felt immediately throughout the country. It was like aftershocks radiating from the epicenter of a violent earthquake. By November 1930, Howard personally felt the impact of the Great Depression for the first time. The Bank of Italy which employed him merged with the Bank of America of California. The merged bank took the name Bank of America National Trust and Savings Association. Following this merger, Howard was employed by the First Exchange State Bank as the assistant cashier at one of its four branches. This employment continued for only fourteen months, when in January 1932, the bank was placed in receivership for liquidation. This tough blow, coming only seven months after their marriage, introduced Howard and Claire to two years of trauma and struggle as they tried to stem the tide of economic adversity which the Great Depression had heaped upon them. There were no jobs available even for willing and able workers like Howard Hunter. In these dire circumstances he had to improvise. He accepted any honorable work which was available and used his entrepreneurial skills to invent jobs.

The novelty and variety of what he did to make ends meet is quite astonishing. He negotiated a credit agreement to buy supplies and equipment, including coin wrappers and adding machines, from the receiver of the bank and resold them to other banks, repaying the receiver when he collected. He and his father-in-law produced bronzed statues and bookends for sale to visitors at the 1932 Olympic Summer Games held in Los Angeles. Their product was beautiful, but the depression economy put a damper on sales. He purchased granulated soap and liquid bleach in large lots, repackaging it in small containers which he sold door-to-door. He noted it was unpleasant, tedious work, "but I was able to make enough to pay the rent and buy groceries." For some time he worked for the receiver which was liquidating the First Exchange State Bank. He had to resign because of a conflict of interest when the receiver included him in a stockholders liability suit. (He owned a few shares of the bank's stock.) He was employed for a while by the Works Progress Administration at thirty cents an hour constructing a storm drain. After seven days on the job he received a check for fourteen dollars and seventy cents. "Again we were saved from starvation." In the summer of 1933, he worked for his father-in-law, Jacob Jeffs, who had a contract to paint the structural steel on four new bridges. The remote location of the bridges made it necessary to camp out. Claire did the cooking for the crew which also included her brother, Ellsworth.

Not long after this job was completed, Jacob died unexpectedly while on a business trip to Utah. His body was returned to California for burial. Martha was comforted in her bereavement, for a few months earlier, Claire and Howard had accepted the invitation to move into the Jeffs family home as a further means of economy as they strove to fight the Depression.

CHAPTER FIVE

New Horizons—The University

In January 1934, a few months after finishing the bridge-painting job, a life-changing opportunity opened up for Howard. He was hired by the Los Angeles County Flood Control District to work in its real estate division. His duties entailed handling a variety of matters involving real estate transactions, conveyances, contracts, title searches, mortgages and other title encumbrances, and eminent domain proceedings. He found the work challenging and satisfying. Moreover, it introduced him to court proceedings as he assisted attorneys in preparing cases and had the opportunity from time to time to participate as a paralegal in court.

This experience turned his attention toward a career he had never considered before—an attorney-at-law. Was it feasible to aim toward such a goal? Scholastically he was ill-prepared to undertake it. He had had no university training. Counting the required undergraduate courses and then graduate-level legal studies, he would be looking at a minimum of five academic years of concentrated study. He was in his twenty-seventh year, married, and Claire was expecting their first child. Except for the brief banking courses he had taken, it had been eight years since he had been involved in concentrated classroom studies. This meant he would be competing with younger students who did not have the myriad responsibilities of a family man trying to maintain his balance during a major economic depression. Finally, to cap the daunting list of reasons why he should not make the attempt, Howard and Claire Hunter had no money, which meant he would have to work full-time to maintain his family and study at night.

Given Howard Hunter's self-confidence and his proven record of success in high school, in Scouting, in the ROTC, and with the Croonaders, it does not appear that this was a difficult decision for him to make. He seems to have regarded it as a rare window of opportunity which could lead him into the professional class with its attendant financial and social rewards. With his growing knowledge of the gospel and his increased ability and desire to serve, we cannot discount the presence of spiritual influences and motivations in this mix which helped to bring about his decision to go for it.

It was fortunate for Howard that there was a good university in Los Angeles, Southwestern, which offered night classes and a path to graduation from an accredited law school. In counseling with the admissions office, he learned that because he had no prior university training, it would be necessary to complete certain basic undergraduate courses as a condition to entering law school. It was projected that if all went well with his studies, he could be qualified to enter law school in a year and a half, or by the autumn of 1935. Once Howard's Boise High School credits were received and cleared and the necessary financial arrangements were completed, Howard was admitted as a first-quarter freshman to Southwestern University. Thus began the most intense and pressure-filled five-year period in Howard W. Hunter's life. During this period he learned and mastered the juggler's art—the art of keeping all the balls in the air. His responsibilities required a major adjustment in his scheduling. During these five years, every minute counted.

Near the time Howard began his studies at Southwestern University, an event occurred which further complicated his crowded schedule, yet which gave him joys he had not experienced before. On March 20, 1934, Howard William Hunter Jr. was born. As adults, neither Howard nor Claire had ever had a small baby in their home. It was a miraculous, supernal event for them. To consider they had literally become one with each other through the birth of this infant filled them with awe, especially as they reflected on the eternal significance of the event. Because of their temple sealing, there would be an eternal relationship between them and their child. Suddenly the concepts of family life on earth and eternal relationships took on new meaning.

Just as sudden was their awakening to the earthly duties of parenthood. The baby had to be fed, bathed, and diapered regularly. None of these services could be postponed, nor was Howard Jr. amenable to a fixed schedule. The required services had to be provided when he needed them. This could be at any time of the day or night, according to his whim. The parents raised no objection to the demands of this new, benign dictator in their midst. Indeed, they responded to them with servile alacrity. Still, the baby did present new scheduling and financial problems to which his parents willingly adjusted. With these adjustments came an appreciation for the appealing personality unfolding before their eyes. They watched with avid interest every movement or expression of the baby which reflected intelligence or physical aptitude. They commented on his smile, the way he reached out for them, and later on his first babbling words, his ability to roll over, to crawl, and then to walk his first halting steps. These were major achievements in the baby's development, frequently discussed and extolled by his parents.

In late summer, his parents saw a marked change in Billy's conduct. He acted tired and withdrawn, so unlike his usual happy self. Concerned, they consulted a doctor who said the baby was anemic and prescribed a transfusion; his father supplied the needed blood. A brief improvement in their son's condition was followed by a relapse which required hospitalization. Here Howard gave more blood. Nothing helped their baby. Finally, the little boy was placed in a special children's hospital where a battery of tests revealed that the loss of blood was caused by an intestinal ulcer. The hospital staff recommended surgery. Howard lay nearby his son, giving more blood as the doctors operated. The results were inconclusive. The worried parents, who remained at their baby's bedside for three days and nights, were finally persuaded to return home to get some rest. Soon they received a call advising he was worse. They returned and were sitting at his bedside when little Billy slipped away on October 11, 1934. "We were grief-stricken and numb as we left the hospital into the night," wrote Howard. They were comforted by a lovely funeral service and by their knowledge of the favored eternal status of an infant who dies before reaching the age of accountability.

The full impact of their baby's passing did not occur until some time after the funeral. The impact was more severe upon Claire than upon Howard, who had to focus immediately upon his job and the university. She, however, had only an empty nest which daily reminded her of the beautiful child who was lost to them. In order to avoid morbid thoughts and at the same time to bolster the family's financial status, Claire decided to return to work. She readily found employment at Bullock's Department Store, which had taken over Blackstones.

Howard forged ahead with his schooling. It was not easy. He was not competing on a level playing field with his fellow students. Most of them were much younger than he; nor did most of them have family responsibilities as he did. Then too, his long absence from the classroom had dulled his study habits. Unsettling thoughts about Billy's illness and death were not helpful. In these circumstances, it would have been easy to give up and to quit. After all, university training is not essential to happiness and success. That can be obtained by living the gospel. Consider that several of the early Presidents of the Church were without university training—Joseph Smith, Brigham Young, John Taylor, Wilford Woodruff, Joseph F. Smith, and Heber J. Grant. Among these, Lorenzo Snow was the only exception, and he attended Oberlin College but briefly. Beyond that, Howard's ancestors had lived useful, happy lives without university training. Why then should he continue along this tortuous path? Why not go along as before and be happy, free of all this pressure? Given his analytical mind, it is easy to think of him going through this mental process as he evaluated his life at this crucial time. We know the outcome as he returned to his studies with a vengeance following the death of his beloved son. There is no precise blueprint of his study habits at the university. We only know that he was persistent and that he was successful. Through five long years, in good times and in bad, through sickness and health, through life and death, he strove mightily to obtain his education. His persistence was remarkable and his success was admirable.

During the first year and a half of his university classes, Howard took the basic undergraduate courses. For the most part, these entailed learning and sometimes memorizing basic facts and concepts. These were interesting, sometimes entertaining, and provided a better understanding of the world about him and of his role in it. They hardly prepared him for what he encountered in the fall quarter of 1935, when he began taking classes in law school, beginning with contracts, torts, and property law.

He soon discovered the vast difference between undergraduate studies and law school. It was unsettling to learn that there was no fixed and certain answer to a question put by a law professor in an examination. Such questions were phrased so as to enable the professor to learn whether the student knew the law and its principles and, perhaps more important, whether the student had the ability to apply the law convincingly to a complex set of facts. Howard and his fellow students were also stressed to discover they were to learn the legal principles in a particular field of the law by studying actual cases compiled in their textbooks. This underscored the reality that the role of a lawyer is essentially adversarial. Whether in court or at the office preparing contracts, legal briefs, or giving advice, a lawyer faces either an actual or a potential adversary who may challenge what has been written or said. There was a basic core of competitiveness in Howard Hunter such that he approached these studies with genuine enthusiasm.

Another shock for the new law school student was to learn that examinations would not cover merely short segments of a course but would cover material extending over an entire quarter or more. Thus, a student's entire grade would depend upon a single examination given at the end. This procedure created enormous pressure and uncertainty in the mind of the student which was increased by reports of the high dropout rate among law school students. Law school administrators and faculty justified this demanding system on the premise that it was the best way to prepare lawyers to face the rigors of a tough, competitive profession. In the process, they washed out those thought to lack the stamina or acumen to be successful at the law. Law school administrators found further justification for this system in the rigid examinations given by the state bar association to law school graduates who sought to be admitted to practice in California courts. A high rate of failure among the graduates of a particular law school could tarnish its reputation or might even invite scrutiny into its accreditation.

These were the conditions which existed at the Southwestern University Law School when Howard began his studies there in the fall of 1935. He faced a daunting task. Except for the prayers and faith of Claire and their extended families and his reliance upon the Lord, he faced it alone. As suggested already, it was imperative to budget his time rigorously. Only so much time could be allocated to each course during the day. If that were insufficient, it still had to do. To take more time for one course would only shortchange another. He followed this strict regimen with unswerving diligence until the first week in June 1939. He graduated cum laude, ranked third in his class. He was only two tenths of 1 percent behind the student ranked first and one tenth of 1 percent behind the student ranked second. Commencement exercises were held June 8, 1939, in the Hollywood Memorial Auditorium.

It was a signal achievement by any standard one may wish to apply. At age thirty-one he had acquired an educational status which would change his life forever. It was something which could never be taken away from him. It was something to celebrate. And he and Claire did celebrate in their own way—for a week. There still loomed ahead one major obstacle before he could legitimately call himself a professional man. This was the California State Bar Association examination, reputed to be one of the toughest in the country. A week after graduation, Howard began a bar review course taught by one of the professors at the university. For several months he reviewed with the professor and other graduates all of the basic legal courses offered by the law school. There was no way of knowing the questions the examiners would ask. Certainly there would be probing questions in the basic subjects: contracts, torts, and property law. Beyond that it was educated guesswork on the part of the professor who had conducted many bar review courses over the years. From that experience the professor could not resist a little gallows humor as the course ended. He told the class that of any three students seated together at the examination, only one would receive a passing grade. Here then was the final filter devised by the leaders of the California Bar to eliminate from the legal profession all but the best of those applying for admission.

The examination was held over a three-day period, October 23–25, 1939. Howard called it "one of the most grinding experiences of my life." One could not avoid thinking of the consequences of failure. To fail would leave him essentially in the same economic status he occupied before enrolling at the university. The degree from the law school would qualify him as a paralegal, but that was his employment status with the City of Los Angeles when he started at Southwestern.

According to the efficient grapevine, there were two kinds of bar examination notifications. Those who had failed received a thin one-page letter of regret. Those who were successful received a letter of congratulation and a sheaf of papers with forms and instructions for being admitted to practice in state and federal courts in

California. So when Claire called Howard at his office on December 12 to tell him he had a letter from the Committee of Bar Examiners, he asked whether the letter was fat or thin. Told it was fat, he recorded later, "I felt a surge of blood to my head and I closed my eyes and waited for her to open and read the letter. The hard work and the sacrifice we had made were at a successful conclusion." The professor who taught the bar review course was correct—of the 718 who took the examination only 254, or 35.4 percent, passed. Howard could take satisfaction not only from passing the bar exam, but that he had competed with graduates from the major law schools in the state: Stanford, UC Berkeley, UCLA, and USC.

It is said the wheels of justice grind very slowly. Howard must have felt the truth of this maxim, given the prolonged process which finally resulted in his being inducted as a full-fledged lawyer. On January 14, 1940, he took the oath of office at ceremonies of the California Supreme Court in Los Angeles. This authorized him to practice law before that court and all California State Courts. On February 5, he was admitted to the bar of the U.S. District Court for Southern California. And on April 8, he was admitted to the bar of the U.S. Court of Appeals for the Ninth Circuit. This completed Howard W. Hunter's induction into California's legal community.

Unlike most newly minted lawyers, Howard had legal work lined up awaiting his admission to the bar. This encouraged him to rent office space in downtown Los Angeles from attorney James R. Bradley. These were minor legal matters, so Howard was able to continue working for the Los Angeles County Flood Control District. Indeed, he worked there part-time until March 1945, when his private practice was firmly established.

CHAPTER SIX

Full Steam Ahead

While law school was the main focus of the Hunter family until 1940, other aspects of their lives had not lain dormant. On May 4, 1936, Claire had given birth to their second son, who was given the name John Jacob Hunter, in recognition of four generations of Hunters who had borne the name John, as well as Claire's father, Jacob Jeffs. The birth of this child did much to assuage the grief caused by the death of Billy two years earlier. Claire especially was comforted by the arrival of baby John, who filled the void created when her first child was taken.

John's arrival sparked a decision his parents had been mulling for some time. They had been living in the Jeffs' home for several years. With the baby expected and Howard's job with the city secure, they had decided to purchase a home. They found a suitable five-room house in Alhambra. Priced at $3600, they acquired it for

$500 down and interest payments of $15 a month with the balance payable in three years. It was located in the Alhambra Ward of the Pasadena Stake. The immediate family of Howard and Claire Hunter was completed on June 29, 1938, when Richard Allen Hunter was born.

When the Hunters first moved into their new home, Howard was heavily occupied with his city job and classes at law school; as a result, his and Claire's social life was practically nil. Because of Howard's responsibilities, his understanding bishop deliberately refrained from giving him Church responsibilities. This situation changed following Howard's graduation from law school. To celebrate, he and Claire left the boys with his parents and drove to San Francisco. There they attended the World's Fair and spent time visiting his ninety-year-old grandfather. A little later, after Howard had passed the bar exam, he was called as the instructor of the junior genealogy class and Claire was called as a teacher in the junior Sunday School.

It was a happy, comparatively relaxing time for them. The grinding discipline of night school and seemingly endless study and class preparations were behind them. Howard's employment with the city and his growing practice provided more than adequate means for their livelihood. Indeed, they had begun to look around for a larger home which would better serve their needs. However, a bombshell exploded in the midst of this scene of domestic tranquility. It occurred on August 27, 1940. At a meeting with Bertrum M. Jones, president of the Pasadena Stake, Howard was called as the bishop of the new El Sereno Ward, to be created by dividing the Alhambra Ward.

Howard was dumbfounded. He had heard no rumors about the division. He was amazed that someone as young as his thirty-two years would be called to a position which, in his experience, had always been filled by much older men. To that date, Howard was the youngest man called as a bishop in Southern California. In retrospect it is easy to see why the stake presidency had nominated him. Earlier he had served in the stake as a Scout leader, and it was known he was an Eagle Scout. His successful struggles to obtain an education and to be admitted to the bar were also known by the stake and ward leaders. And of course his bright, friendly personality was well-known in the area, as also his successful roles as a husband and father. He seemed to be tailor-made for the job.

Five days after the call, on Sunday, September 1, Howard W. Hunter was sustained as the first bishop of the El Sereno Ward. Also sustained were his counselors, Frank Brundage and Richard M. Bleak. He was ordained a high priest and a bishop and was set apart as the bishop a week later by Elder Joseph F. Merrill of the Twelve, who was in Los Angeles to preside at the quarterly conference of the Pasadena Stake—at that time stake presidents were not delegated the authority to ordain bishops. The incident had special significance for Bishop Hunter. It was the first time he had had an Apostle of the Lord lay his hands upon his head.

His association with Elder Merrill continued, and an experience he had later with Elder Merrill forever affected his attitude toward the sacred tithing funds of the Church. At the time, he was serving as the president of the Pasadena Stake and Elder Merrill was the visiting General Authority at the stake conference. At the conclusion of the conference, President Hunter drove Elder Merrill to the train depot and headed toward the Pullman car. The Apostle instead directed him to the chair car, explaining that he would take the chair car to Las Vegas where he would transfer to the Pullman, thereby saving the Church some ten dollars, more or less. As the result of this example of strict economy, President Hunter used great care throughout his Church career in the expenditure of sacred tithing funds.

The manner in which Bishop Hunter went forward with his duties is reminiscent of the humble, faithful way in which he began to tithe and to seek a patriarchal blessing once these principles were made clear to him. At the time of his call by the stake president, and after expressing genuine surprise that one as young as he would be called, he willingly accepted, saying merely, "I will do my best." After being sustained by the members of the ward, he asked the stake presidency what he was supposed to do. He was told simply to find a place in which to meet, to organize the ward, and to get going. "This was all new to me, not having served in a bishopric," wrote Howard, "but I followed directions."

Here his experience in negotiating the contract for the Croonaders tour of the Orient fifteen years earlier and his knowledge as a practicing attorney simplified his acquisition of a meeting place. He soon negotiated a contract with the local Masonic lodge to sublet space in the Florence Building in El Sereno. The organization of the ward proceeded apace with the calling and setting apart of officers and teachers in the various organizations and the calling and instructing of a clerical staff to handle the records and financial matters. One of Bishop Hunter's first calls was to Claire Hunter to supervise the junior Sunday School.

Soon after, the Hunters found a suitable new home within the boundaries of the ward at 3419 Winchester Avenue. A three-bedroom home with an unfinished second floor and basement, it was more than adequate for their personal needs and provided a place for many ward social activities which could not be accommodated at their rented space in the Florence Building. One of the bedrooms was fitted out as an office for the bishop where he could conduct interviews and hold council meetings. It is fortunate that at the threshold of his service as a priesthood leader, Bishop Hunter had the experience of building a new ward from the ground up. The knowledge and insights thus gained served him well later as a stake president, as an Apostle, as the President of the Twelve, and as the President of the Church.

Bishop Hunter presided over the El Sereno Ward until November 10, 1946, a period of six years and two months. It was a small ward of only 265 members. It functioned in the manner of a large family. They felt responsible for each other and everyone was loved and needed. In that setting, Bishop Hunter's native leadership skills blossomed. He became a surrogate father to all. His jovial nature put everyone at ease and created a sense of belonging among them. However, an incident near the beginning of his ministry showed him in a different, more authoritarian light. Aaronic Priesthood holders, despite counsel not to, would leave sacrament meeting after they had performed their duties and go to a nearby drugstore fountain for malted milks and other confections. One Sunday, Bishop Hunter decided it was time for a showdown. After they made their usual exit, he suspended the meeting, walked to the drugstore, and told the dumbfounded young men that as soon as they had finished their treats they should return to the chapel where the services would resume. The episode ended all truancy during sacrament meetings. The message was clear—Bishop Hunter is a nice guy, but don't cross him.

• • •

The attack on Pearl Harbor on December 7, 1941, affected the El Sereno Ward heavily. Rumor and fear ruled the day for the residents of Los Angeles. Published reports of Japanese submarines spotted off the West Coast created a frenzy, resulting in blackouts in the city. The fear was so widespread that trains entering California from the east were required to shade their windows. Guards were posted at all crossing points. A wartime mentality settled on the Golden State as the draft took most able-bodied men into the military. Food shortages ultimately brought on rationing. A sense of urgency and uncertainty affected all.

As an ordained minister, Bishop Hunter was immune from the draft. He rallied ward members to lend support to those families whose husbands and sons were at war. The drain on male leadership in the ward caused by the draft imposed heavier responsibilities upon those who remained. This prompted the bishop to assume direct leadership of the Scouting program. For two years he led his Scouts in their quest for merit badges and awards, taking them on overnight camping trips where field training was given in survival techniques.

When Church leaders placed a moratorium on the construction of new chapels during the war, Bishop Hunter led out in drives for a ward building fund, anticipating the end of the war. El Sereno became known as the "onion project ward" as the members worked at a pickle factory trimming onions. Their compensation went into the building fund. The fulfillment of an assignment at the pickle factory was determined by smell, not by report. Seemingly partial to odorous jobs, El Sereno members later hired out to shred cabbage at a sauerkraut plant. Then, taking Howard's Depression initiative of repackaging and selling bulk soap as an example, ward members repackaged and sold Kix breakfast cereal, which Bishop Hunter purchased by the carload.

• • •

While Claire's niece, Lee Jeffs, attended Woodbury College in Los Angeles, she was a frequent visitor in the Hunter home. When Lee and her fellow students sought to organize a Deseret Club (an organization for campuses too small for an institute), they were told it would be necessary to obtain an outside sponsor. Despite his heavy duties with the city, his private practice, his service as bishop, and his role as the head of an active family, Howard yielded to Lee's request that he sponsor their club. This entailed attending Wednesday noon meetings for a year where he taught the students from *Jesus the Christ* by Elder James E. Talmage.

Later Bishop Hunter found occasion to call upon Lee to redeem her debt to him for his sponsorship of the Deseret Club. During one of her visits, Howard asked her as a favor to accompany a young man from his ward to a Church-sponsored Sweetheart Ball. With tongue in cheek he told her the young man was short, homely, and awkward but pleaded with her to be nice to him. Expecting the worst, Lee was happily surprised to find the young man, Richard Harrison Child, was tall and handsome. Howard and Claire accompanied them to the dance, and three years later Bishop Hunter performed their civil marriage. The next day Claire traveled with them to the Mesa Temple where they were sealed for time and eternity. Thus the term "certifiable matchmaker" must be added to Bishop Hunter's long list of personal qualities.

On November 10, 1946, Howard W. Hunter was released as the bishop of the El Sereno Ward. This ended the first segment of his training for the apostleship. He could look back on the experience with a justifiable sense of satisfaction. He had performed well under difficult circumstances. "I will always be thankful for this privilege and the education of these years," he wrote later. "They were difficult in many ways, and particularly hard on Claire, but she never once complained, and we were grateful for the values it brought to our family." A final accolade to his service came years later when former members of the El Sereno Ward would tell him by word or by letter of the profound influence for good he had exerted upon them through his service as their bishop. These voluntary expressions of gratitude were a remarkable fulfillment of the special blessing conferred upon him by his stake patriarch, Joseph A. West, at the very beginning of his service as bishop. Said the patriarch: "You shall be known as an honest, just, and honorable bishop among the members of [your] ward—and in future years, these members will come to you with tears in their eyes and thank you for your blessings and your guiding hand and the administration of the work you are now called upon to do."

CHAPTER SEVEN

An Interval of Peace

On the day he was released as the bishop, November 10, 1946, Howard was called as the president of the high priests quorum of the Pasadena Stake. This was a call of considerable significance. Unlike today, when a stake president concurrently serves as the president of the high priests quorum, at that time the president of the high priests quorum presided ecclesiastically over the stake president and all other high priests in the stake—including counselors in the stake presidency, high councilors, and bishoprics. It was this duplication of effort which later resulted in a stake president also being set apart as the president of the high priests quorum. In any event, Howard's call to this position was considered to be one of importance, perhaps signaling that this young leader, still in his thirties, was destined for high Church responsibility.

While this new calling was important, it was far less

demanding than was his role as the bishop. Specifically, it was far less "time-consuming," as Howard phrased it. A major responsibility of the stake high priest quorum was to provide nurturing services to members of the Church in the Los Angeles County General Hospital. Among other things, this entailed Thursday evening assignments for the high priests to administer blessings to these members. It was also the responsibility of Brother Hunter and his counselors to see that the high priest groups in the various wards of the stake were properly organized and functioning, providing necessary instruction and counseling for their members and families. But with his counselors, group leaders in each ward in the stake, and many high priests in each group, this assignment occupied very little of President Hunter's time compared to the daily efforts required to direct the affairs of an active ward. He was to enjoy this period of relative peace and quiet for four years, during which time he became more involved in the activities of his family, assuming many of the responsibilities Claire had handled so ably and uncomplainingly throughout his years as bishop.

In 1948 the Hunters moved to the last home they would occupy while living in California. It was a new, ranch-style home located in Arcadia. It had three bedrooms—a master bedroom suite for Howard and Claire and a bedroom for each of the boys. Nearby were the library, living room, dining room, and kitchen. The house was separated from the garage by a breezeway behind which was a guest room which opened onto a patio.

During the nine years Brother Hunter served as the stake president, this guest room was used to accommodate General Authorities who visited Los Angeles for stake conferences. At the time, stake conferences were held each quarter. Over the nine-year period of his service, President and Sister Hunter hosted many of the General

Authorities in their home, thereby creating strong bonds of friendship and understanding. It is a curious fact that, generally speaking, the presidents of stakes that live away from the headquarters of the Church become better acquainted with the General Authorities on a personal level than do the stake presidents residing in Salt Lake City. It is a rare thing for a stake president in Salt Lake City to receive a General Authority into his home to stay overnight. Their association is usually limited to the various meetings connected with the conference. Under these circumstances, it is likely that when he was called to the apostleship, President Hunter was better known to the General Authorities than were most of the stake presidents then residing near Church headquarters.

At the time of Howard's release as bishop, his sons John and Richard were ten and eight years old, respectively. It is unlikely they had more than a scanty recollection, as small children four years of age and under, of family life before their father became the bishop. In their view, it must have seemed he had always been their bishop. As bishop, Howard had been anxious to set the proper example for his ward and so was diligent in leading his family in their prayers, scripture study, and Church attendance. Moreover, the family observed one night a week as a family night, although at the time this was not an extensively followed practice in the Church. This afforded the opportunity for discussion, not only about gospel topics but about the parents' life experiences. This was enhanced by family prayers and discussions at the dinner table.

In such a setting, the Hunter boys were securely anchored to their family and to the Church from an early age. During their first years while Howard was busy with bishop's duties and building his legal practice, Claire played the leading role in training and directing their sons. After his release as bishop and call as high priest quorum president, Brother Hunter was pleased to assume full responsibility in this process. Soon after acquiring their new home in Arcadia, Howard and his sons began to convert the guest room into a miniature train depot with intertwined tracks, stop and go signals, signs, and spur sidings. They delighted in each new acquisition of a locomotive or cars, some with bells, whistles, and flashing lights. It was an absorbing pastime for them, made more realistic by visiting the local train depot, studying its makeup, and altering their model to correspond with reality. It was a sad day, indeed, when after Howard's call as stake president, they dismantled the model depot in order to prepare the guest room for use by visiting General Authorities.

In 1951 John and Richard took diving lessons at the Pasadena City College from Colleen Hutchins, a Latter-day Saint, who later was crowned Miss America. This interest in aquatics gave rise to the installation of a swimming pool in the patio area and the construction of a four-room poolside deck house. Two of the rooms were for dressing, one housed the pool maintenance equipment, and the fourth was a tool room and workshop for Howard. These facilities not only provided a wonderful athletic outlet for the entire family, but were also a delightful setting for social activities.

Both Howard and Claire were active in assisting their sons in the quest for merit badges as they worked toward their Eagle Scout award, which both of them ultimately received. A memorable experience for Howard was John's quest for a merit badge which required that he sleep fifty nights in the open. Some of them were fulfilled when father and both sons slept in the Los Angeles Arboretum, a heavily wooded area where some Tarzan movies were filmed. An overnight stay in the Mojave Desert was the most memorable of all when the three frightened campers, suddenly awakened by the thunderous sound of a train which seemed to be bearing down upon them, scrambled from their sleeping bags. Making camp in the darkening evening, they had failed to notice their campsite lay in a direct line from the train tracks which then veered away fairly close to their camp. While Howard was genuinely pleased to assist his sons in their Scouting adventures, he was "glad when the fifty were completed."

Later the three intrepid Scouters collaborated in making kayaks for a float down the Rogue River in Oregon. They made successful practice runs on the estuary of the Los Angeles River at Long Beach. However, on the rugged Rogue River, they experienced a near-tragedy when Richard became trapped underneath his overturned kayak. Fortunately he was rescued, scared but unscathed. That night as they rested on a sandbar, Howard comforted them by retelling the story of Job.

The achievements of these two noble sons are a testament to the nurturing love and dedication of their parents. They were faithful and obedient as they progressed through various milestones in their Church activity. They were successful in their high school experience, both excelling academically; John being recognized in athletics and Richard in forensics. Both served honorable missions in Australia, at the conclusion of which, Howard and Claire met them and then accompanied them on a special tour around the world. Both were graduates of major law schools, John from USC and Richard from UC Berkeley. John became a judge in Southern California and Richard a successful attorney in San Jose. Both were married in the temple to worthy and accomplished women with whom they raised exemplary families. Both were ordained bishops at age thirty-two, the same young age their father became a bishop. Both served in stake presidencies. In the summer of 2008, at age chard was called as a temple president. It is undoubtedly to President and Sister Hunter any personal achievements lades received during their lives pale in comparison to the ho[illegible] of being the parents of this family.

The growth and development of such a family does not occur by chance. It requires much thought, prayer, and persistence. That such elements were at the core in the development of the Howard W. Hunter family is evident from this "objective of life" composed by Howard near the time of his service as the president of the high priests quorum of the Pasadena Stake: "It is my aim to find pleasure and enjoyment in life by seeking after those things which are good and worthwhile, that I may gain knowledge and wisdom with each passing year; to carefully plan my allotted time so that none of it will be wasted; to give my family the benefits of education, recreation, and travel; to conduct my life in obedience to the Gospel of Jesus Christ; to so manage my business affairs that I will have an income adequate to provide my family with their wants and the advantages of some of the finer things in life; and to set aside a portion for investment to provide an income for retirement."

CHAPTER EIGHT

President of the Pasadena Stake

By February 1950, it had become an unwritten maxim in the Church that when two Apostles were assigned to attend a stake conference, it meant the stake presidency would be reorganized. So when the presidency of the Pasadena Stake received word that Elders Stephen L Richards and Harold B. Lee of the Twelve would attend their stake conference on February 25–26, the grapevine in the stake began to buzz about the identity of the new stake president. It was discovered that the two Apostles had a much broader agendum than was suspected; they were there to divide the stake, whose membership had grown to over 9,000. As the president of the high priests quorum in the stake, Howard was interviewed by the two Apostles, together with the stake presidency, high councilors, bishops, and others specially requested by the visitors. Following these interviews, and after fervent prayer, forty-two-year-old Howard W. Hunter was called as the president of the Pasadena Stake. Fauntleroy L. Hunsaker, former first counselor in the Pasadena Stake presidency, was called as the president of the new East Los Angeles Stake. The stake over which President Hunter would preside consisted of 4,482 members in six wards. However, very soon afterward, two of these wards were divided. President Hunter selected Daken K. Broadhead and A. Kay Berry as his counselors. By the time of their first stake conference in May 1950, the Pasadena Stake "was well organized and settled down."

Howard's new calling was a great shock to both him and Claire; it was so sudden and unexpected. They spent many hours discussing its implications and its probable effect upon their family life. One aspect of it gave them special concern—their role of hosting visiting General Authorities in their home. They had never had a personal relationship with a General Authority before, men so highly respected and revered. It took some time to adjust to the idea of receiving them into their home on a personal basis. Once this concern was resolved, they moved forward with confidence. Their first decision was to convert the guest room into special quarters for visiting General Authorities. This entailed removing the miniature train track and accessories and storing the cars and locomotives. It was a sacrifice Howard and his sons made willingly.

The first General Authority to visit the Pasadena Stake after Howard became its president was Elder Marion G. Romney, Assistant to the Twelve. He came for the quarterly stake conference in May 1950 and became the first General Authority to occupy the Hunter's special room overlooking the patio. With his down-to-earth demeanor and friendliness, Elder Romney immediately put the Hunters at ease. Moreover, their conversation revealed the visitor's background was similar to that of President

Hunter. Like Howard, Elder Romney was an attorney who had had to struggle for an education. And, like Howard, he had served both as a bishop and a stake president. The friendship thus formed gave President Hunter confidence of a positive and helpful relationship with Church headquarters in Salt Lake City, a confidence which was magnified the following year when on October 11, 1951, Elder Romney was sustained as a member of the Quorum of the Twelve Apostles. It is intriguing to note that following President Romney's death on May 20, 1988, Elder Hunter succeeded him as the President of the Quorum of the Twelve Apostles. As to President Hunter's feeling of closeness to the Church administration in Salt Lake City due to his relationship with Elder Romney, it is interesting that on April 9, 1951, Elder Stephen L Richards, the senior Apostle who presided at his installation as stake president, was sustained as the first counselor in the First Presidency. Thus, when matters pertaining to the Pasadena Stake were discussed in the councils of the First Presidency and Quorum of the Twelve, President Hunter knew there were two members of that council who knew him personally, a fact which was encouraging to him.

Once established and functioning as the stake president, President Hunter soon became aware of a vast difference between that role and his role as a bishop. The main aspect of that difference was that as the stake president he had much more autonomy than before. As a bishop, his presiding officer, the stake president, was always nearby, in the neighborhood as it were, to whom he was constantly accountable. As stake president, however, he was accountable only to the General Authorities of the Church who ordinarily visited him only once every three months. This gave the stake president free rein to take steps deemed necessary to fill local needs, provided they fell within the broad guidelines of Church policy.

It was not long after being installed in office that President Hunter and his counselors began to focus on a local need. This was a perceived fragmentation among families in the stake, resulting in a decrease in spirituality. There were so many things going on and so many things to attract the attention of the youth that the parents seemed to be losing control of the family agenda. As President Hunter and his counselors discussed and prayed about this issue, conferring with bishops and others in the stake, they came up with this solution: establish Monday night of each week as a family night, with the lights in church buildings in the stake being turned off and no meetings being scheduled. This program was adopted in the Pasadena Stake and was followed during the years President Hunter served as the stake president. As the program rolled out, the parents were urged to be creative in planning their family home evenings, combining prayerful gospel study with interesting and appropriate recreational activities. In 1965, six years after Elder Hunter was called to the Twelve, the family home evening program was adopted as a worldwide program of the Church (see *Story of the Latter-day Saints*, 599).

In the early 1950s, Southern California was perhaps the fastest-growing area in the Church. This entailed heavy expense in providing buildings and other accommodations for the rapidly growing Church population. Less than four months after being called as the stake president, Howard was initiated into the financial responsibilities of his new calling. The presidents of ten stakes in the area were asked to raise $100,000 as a down payment on the purchase of a five-hundred-acre ranch at Perres, California, and to pay the balance of $350,000 over five years. Howard willingly joined with the other stake presidents in fulfilling this request without knowing exactly how this acquisition fit into their programs. Then, at general conference in October 1951, the presidents of the now-fourteen stakes were asked to raise $1 million to assist in building the Los Angeles Temple. Six months later it was reported these stakes had pledged $1.6 million for this purpose. Then on October 11, 1952, in the midst of these significant efforts, President Hunter undertook an action which would involve him in an even more expensive and time-consuming Church project. On that day he broke ground for a new stake center for the Pasadena Stake located on a two-and-a-half-acre site on a hillside overlooking the San Gabriel Valley. Of this event President Hunter reported: "This was the commencement of a huge undertaking with many problems and time-consuming supervision that only bishops and stake presidents can understand."

Unlike today, members of the Pasadena Stake at that time were asked to pay, over and above their usual tithing and offerings, part of the cost of constructing the stake center. The responsibility to raise these funds lay chiefly on President Hunter. On one occasion when local funds to cover current labor and material costs had run low, President Hunter learned an important lesson about raising funds among members of the Church. He called a priesthood group together and explained the predicament the stake was in. He then sat back and waited. Soon members of the group began to volunteer contributions until the money needed had been raised. From that moment, there was always sufficient money available to cover expenses. The perception which emerged from this meeting was that all members of the Church share responsibility for the work to be accomplished regardless of their position.

Guidelines adopted by the building department in Salt Lake City placed limitations on the amounts to be expended for different items. President Hunter worked around these requirements to provide items he felt needful for the local congregation. He acquired a Wurlitzer organ from a local theater for the stake center chapel instead of the electric organ authorized by the Church building department. Olive trees which cost $350 each were used in landscaping the grounds although the building department allocated only thirty dollars per tree. Ever after these were known as the "Howard Hunter olive trees."

Labor provided by members of the stake in the construction was credited against the local share of construction costs, so members of the stake were involved in various aspects of construction, the stake president providing more than his share of manual labor. About a hundred men wielded wheelbarrows during the day of the "great pour" when, from early morning until evening, cement was poured for the building's walls. When the roof was to be installed, a block-long line of workers—men, women, and children—passed tiles from the ground to the roof.

June 4, 1954, was a day of special significance in Howard's tenure as the president of the Pasadena Stake. On that day more than fifteen hundred members of the Church gathered to participate in the dedication of the new Pasadena stake center. Those who could not find seating in the chapel or the adjacent cultural hall were seated in various rooms of the 25,000-square-foot building to which the proceedings were carried by direct audio feed. Significantly and appropriately, the General Authority who was present to dedicate the building was Stephen L Richards, First Counselor in the First Presidency of the Church. The last time President Richards had presided at a meeting in the Pasadena Stake was the occasion when he and Elder Harold B. Lee had selected Howard W. Hunter as the stake president. Now, four years later, President Richards could witness some of the accomplishments of President Hunter, vindicating as it were the judgment of Howard's call as the stake president. For President Hunter, the dedication was the culmination of months of stress and strain as he and his leadership team and several members of the stake worked through the myriad problems connected with the completion of the building. He wrote: "It was a thrilling event for those of us who had worked so hard for this accomplishment."

This occasion provided another opportunity for a General Authority from Salt Lake City to appraise the character and competence of a promising young leader serving away from the center of the Church. A principal role of the General Authorities is to find and to cultivate leaders. As these men travel throughout the world, they are constantly on the alert to identify those who have leadership potential. Their findings are shared with their brethren as they gather at Church headquarters. As others visit places where prospective leaders have been identified, inquiry is made as to their progress and their readiness to assume roles of responsibility in the ongoing work of the Church. The process is not unlike that of the prudent husbandman who constantly observes the growth of his crops and determines the sequence of harvesting them according to their maturity.

Another of the many General Authorities who stayed in the Hunter home was President J. Reuben Clark Jr., Second Counselor in the First Presidency. On the last day of his stay, President Clark fell while in the guest room, cracking a rib and cutting his head. He was treated by the Hunters' physician before returning home. Several months later, when Howard and Claire traveled to Salt Lake City to attend general conference, President Clark invited them to spend the night in his home in the Avenues. After dinner, the host showed his guests many of the choice documents and mementos he had collected in his years of service as a diplomat and international counselor. These were housed in a two-storey library, whose four walls were lined with President Clark's extensive collection of books and manuscripts. The Hunters slept in a bedroom adjacent to the president's storied library, pictures of which had intrigued members of the Church over the years.

As the Church population in the Southern California area increased dramatically, the General Authorities found it necessary to create a regional council of stake presidents. The purpose of the council was to correlate Church activities whose scope and purpose required overall supervision, such as welfare matters and youth activities. Soon after his call as stake president, Howard was called as the chairman of the Southern California regional council. In its function and purpose, this council assignment was similar to the office of regional representative, which was created later. President Hunter did not preside over the other stake presidents in the region but merely coordinated the Church functions carried on by the council. This call was another recognition of President Hunter's growing leadership capacity and of the high regard in which he was held by the General Authorities in Salt Lake City.

The area included in this region extended from San Luis Obispo on the north to the Mexican border on the south. It included twelve stakes, 120 wards, and almost 65,000 members. Within the region were various welfare projects—citrus groves, poultry farms, and canneries. On June 9, 1951, a large, recently remodeled bishops' storehouse complex southeast of downtown Los Angeles was dedicated by President J. Reuben Clark Jr. Traveling with President Clark were three stalwarts in Church welfare: Elders Harold B. Lee, Henry D. Moyle, and Marion G. Romney. This complex included a Deseret Industries operation and other facilities for the Southern California region. The previous day President Hunter had learned why he and the other stake presidents had earlier been asked to purchase the Perris Ranch in Riverside County—it was dedicated on that day as a Church welfare ranch by President Clark.

President Hunter was a hands-on administrator of the regional council. He wrote: "I have never been on a gloomy welfare project. I have climbed trees and picked lemons, peeled fruit, tended boiler, carried boxes, unloaded trucks, cleaned the cannery, and a thousand and one other things, but the things I remember most are the laughing and the singing and the good fellowship of people engaged in the service of the Lord. It is like the little boy who was carrying another boy on his back. 'Isn't he heavy?' someone asked. The little fellow answered, 'No, he's my brother'" (*Relief Society Magazine,* April 1962, 238).

In 1958, the year before President Hunter was called to the Twelve, the Los Angeles regional council approved the construction of a new cannery on the Los Angeles welfare square, to replace three smaller canneries. This unit, the largest cannery in the Church at the time, processed orange juice, turkey, stews, chili, beans, tomatoes, and other commodities grown within the Los Angeles, San Fernando, and Southern California regions.

In August 1954, President Hunter chaired a regional Mutual Improvement Association conference. It was patterned after the annual all-Church MIA June conference and involved youth from the sixteen stakes in the Los Angeles area. It featured a music festival in the Hollywood Bowl, where a chorus of over 1,400 and a seventy-five-piece symphony orchestra entertained an audience of over 17,000. The following night a colorful dance festival was staged in the stadium of the East Los Angeles Junior College. The final event of the conference was held Sunday morning when President David O. McKay addressed a capacity crowd in the Hollywood

Bowl. Meanwhile, throughout the days of the conference, members of the general boards held training meetings with local youth leaders. In the following two years, similar regional MIA conferences were held in Los Angeles, which featured, successively, Presidents Stephen L Richards and J. Reuben Clark Jr.

From Sunday, March 11, through Wednesday, March 14, 1956, the Los Angeles Temple was dedicated. Two dedicatory sessions were held each day. Howard and Claire attended the first session on Sunday morning. "The General Authorities and stake presidents were seated in the stands at the east end of the auditorium," wrote Howard, "and the Mormon Choir of Southern California occupied the west end." Ten days after the final dedicatory session, Howard and several other stake presidents performed vicarious baptisms in the temple, their own children acting as proxies. Howard's son Richard participated in these ordinances. John was away from home attending Brigham Young University. On April 14, 1956, President David O. McKay, Elders Richard L. Evans and Delbert L. Stapley and their wives, and the stake presidents from the temple district and their wives participated in the first endowment session in the Los Angeles Temple.

With the dedication of the Los Angeles Temple and the three highly publicized MIA conferences held annually from 1954 to 1956, The Church of Jesus Christ of Latter-day Saints became prominently and permanently etched upon the public mind of the city of Los Angeles. The temple was located on property once part of the estate of the well-known silent-movie star Harold Lloyd. Adorned with graceful palm trees, the gleaming white temple was spectacularly visible from the busy freeway. The building became a familiar landmark to tens of thousands of commuters who passed the temple each day. Members and nonmembers of the Church seemed to regard it as their own.

Professional and Business Activities

Throughout his service as a stake president, Howard's professional and business interests burgeoned. His intelligence and his precision in speech and writing engendered confidence in his ability as a counselor and advisor. His open personality and his genuine friendliness conveyed a sense of honesty and integrity. These qualities were the foundation of Howard W. Hunter's success as an attorney and counselor-at-law. The word of satisfied clients spread rapidly. If you want an attorney who is able, honest, and reliable—and who won't gouge you with exorbitant fees—this is your man. In the hurly burly of post-war Los Angeles, this man was a jewel. Clients flocked to his door. Of course, it didn't happen overnight. It took several years for Howard's reputation to become known. A signal evidence of that reputation is that during the relatively short period of his legal career, from 1940 to 1959, he provided counsel and direction for more than two dozen corporations by serving on their boards of directors. One of the most significant of these was his service on the board of directors of the Watson Land Company. This company originated from a Mexican land grant, known as the Rancho San Pedro, made to a Mexican national, Manuel Dominguez, before the Treaty of Guadalupe Hidalgo was ratified in 1848. It was this treaty by which the United States acquired most of the state of California and other large tracts of land in the western United States following the Mexican-American War.

Howard's first contact with the Watson Land Company came about through his association with the attorney James P. Bradley, from whom he rented office space at the beginning of his legal career. Mr. Bradley had married a descendant of Manuel Dominguez and was a member of the board of directors of the Watson Land Company. For several years after being admitted to the bar, Howard did legal work for the company referred to him by Mr. Bradley. This introduced Howard to complicated and lucrative legal matters because the holdings of the company included oil refineries, industrial buildings, and other large commercial properties. After four years of association with the company, Howard was invited to become a member of its board of directors on July 24, 1944, in recognition of his legal skills and sound business judgment. The experience Howard gained from helping to direct the complex affairs of this company, and the prestige and monetary rewards which accompanied it were basic to his later success in directing the affairs of numerous other companies. Howard did legal work for this company until he was called to the Twelve in 1959, and remained a member of its board of directors until he became the President of the Church in 1994.

The most significant Church-related service to a board of directors came to Howard in February 1958, when he was elected to the board of directors of the Beneficial Life Insurance Company headquartered in Salt Lake City. This company was owned by the Church. Its officers and the members of its board of directors included men who were General Authorities of the Church. This assignment brought Howard into an even closer association with the General Authorities of the Church. As a board member, he was in a position where his conduct and judgment could be more closely observed and appraised. During the following twenty months, Howard made regular trips to Salt Lake City to confer with the other members of the Beneficial Life board as they developed policies for the company and charted its business path. At the end of this period, in

October 1959, an event occurred which suddenly lifted Howard into a realm and lifestyle he had never planned for nor contemplated.

One of Howard's clients was a real estate broker named Gilles DeFlon, who purchased and sold commercial and domestic properties. Howard prepared the legal documentation involved in these transactions and in some instances cleared the title to properties with title defects. This often entailed court proceedings which Howard handled. Over time the relationship between them progressed from attorney-client to a business partnership. Such was the mutual confidence between them that business arrangements often were handled on a handshake basis. One company they organized was Sisar Oil Corporation, which owned several small oil-producing wells. Another was Rancho Brea Corporation, a development of mobile homes. The partners also acquired cattle feeding operations, which entailed purchasing young heifers and feeding them until they had attained full growth and then selling them on the open market. Success in such an enterprise required care in acquiring good stock and feed, in controlling the health and feeding patterns of the animals, and in studying market trends. Later Howard engaged in similar feeding operations with his sons John and Richard at Lancaster, California.

Elder Hunter continued his business relationship with Mr. DeFlon after his call to the Twelve. In June 1961, they embarked on one of their most ambitious projects. At that time they purchased a 24,000-acre cattle ranch west of Promontory, Utah. Howard enjoyed visiting this property from time to time. Meanwhile, he handled business matters connected with the operation, including the preparation of tax returns. Following the death of Gilles DeFlon in 1966, Elder Hunter continued the partnership arrangement with Mr. DeFlon's son, James. In 1991, while serving as the President of the Quorum of the Twelve Apostles, President Hunter visited the Promontory Ranch with his partner, James DeFlon. Of the occasion he wrote: "Counting the cows, bulls and heifers, we have about 1,800 head on the ranch and 20 men were working the branding and vaccinations. Jim took me for a ride around the ranch to see the watering tanks and the windmill and the solar pumps that feed the pipelines. It has been a long time since I have seen the ranch and I was amazed at the size of the operation."

As Howard began to make regular trips to Salt Lake City as a member of the Beneficial Life Insurance Company's board, and with so many other business and professional matters pressing upon him, it became apparent he needed help in his law office. Until this time, early 1958, he had worked as a solo practitioner. By happenstance, he received a telephone call at the time from Gordon L. Lund, a young attorney who lived in the Pasadena Stake, asking if Howard knew of an attorney who would like to join him in the practice of law, his associate having recently passed away. Since Gordon Lund was a graduate of the Stanford Law School, had practiced successfully for several years, and had legal experience with a major oil and gas company, this appeared to be a fortuitous solution to Howard's problem. As a result, the law firm of Hunter and Lund came into existence in the early part of 1958. With a partner in the office, along with his efficient secretary, Donna Dain, who had been with him since 1952, Howard felt comfortable in being away from his office. Such was his comfort level that Howard decided in the summer of 1958 to take the first lengthy vacation of his life. On July 2, 1958, Howard, Claire, and Richard departed from the Los Angeles International Airport destined for Australia. Earlier, Richard had received his mission call to serve in Australia, and Howard had received permission from the Missionary Department to accompany him there and to pick up John, who was completing his mission in that land. They flew first to Hawaii, where they spent several days before flying to Fiji, to New Zealand, and then to Australia. After greeting John and saying good-bye to Richard, the Hunters began a two-month journey which would take them the rest of the way around the world. Howard had always had a yen for travel, which was hardly satiated by the Croonader tour to the Orient. Now with means, leisure time, and health, they embarked upon an adventure that few have experienced. Going north first, they made stops in Manila and Hong Kong before touring southeast Asia, stopping in Thailand, Cambodia, and Burma. They visited India and Pakistan before heading into the heart of the Middle East: Israel, Egypt, and Turkey. They stopped in Greece, Italy, Switzerland, and France before touring England, where they were privileged to attend the dedication of the London Temple. Little did Howard realize upon returning to Pasadena that he had just had a preview of what the future held for him in terms of world travel.

Before completing his career as an attorney, Howard had one other service to perform. He acted as matchmaker for his secretary, Donna Dain, whom he introduced to Karl Snow, one of John's friends. In January 1960, shortly after being sustained as a member of the Twelve, he performed the sealing for this couple in the Salt Lake Temple, the first of hundreds he would perform as an Apostle.

CHAPTER NINE

CALL TO THE QUORUM OF THE TWELVE

After recovering from the jet lag of their country-hopping travels, the Hunter family settled into their normal routines. John returned to Provo, Utah, to resume his undergraduate studies at Brigham Young University while his mother took up her studies at the Pasadena City College. Howard still had his day job and his night job—legal and business work during the day and Church work at night as he directed the affairs of a large, active stake. Life was good, filled with daily joys, challenges, and rich promises for the future.

On December 27, 1958, a new era was opened in the lives of Howard and Claire Hunter. On that day their son John was sealed in the Los Angeles Temple to Louine Berry, the daughter of A. Kay Berry, a former counselor to President Hunter in the Pasadena Stake presidency. Following the festivities connected with their marriage, the young couple returned to BYU to continue their studies.

After the extraordinary events of 1958, and reflecting a sense of anticipation for a quieter lifestyle, Howard noted at the beginning of the new year, "After the rush of the holidays, 1959 commenced with what appeared to be a quiet year." Little did he know what life-changing events he would experience in this year. First, John and Louine presented him and Claire with their first grandchild, Robert Mark Hunter, on September 17. Then three weeks later came the wholly unexpected events of the October general conference.

Howard flew to Salt Lake City on Friday, October 9, 1959, in the company of Bishop Eric J. Smith of the East Pasadena Ward, Claire having traveled there a week earlier to visit their new grandson. They arrived after 10:00 A.M., thus missing part of the opening session of the October general conference. Following the session, Howard walked across the street to the Hotel Utah where he found his counselor Daken Broadhead waiting for him. "He told me that Sister Clare Middlemiss, secretary to President McKay, had been looking for me and had asked him to have me come to the office of President McKay as soon as possible." When Howard failed to exhibit any sense of surprise at this information, Daken Broadhead reminded him there was a vacancy in the Twelve. "I know you are joking with me," said Howard. "The First Presidency has asked me to secure some information for them and I presume they want a report." So saying, he walked next door to the Church Administration Building where Sister Middlemiss ushered him into President McKay's office. The prophet wasted no time as the afternoon session of the conference was to begin soon. "President McKay greeted me with a pleasant smile and a warm handshake and then said to me, 'Sit down, President Hunter, I want to talk with you. The Lord has spoken. You are called to be one of his special witnesses, and tomorrow you will be sustained as a member of the Council of the Twelve.'" Howard was dumbfounded. He could not speak. Tears filled his eyes. He was humbled and felt inadequate to the task. He was comforted, though, by the encouraging words of the prophet, who told him of the joys which would come from apostolic service and of the satisfactions which would come from mingling with his brethren of the Twelve. And finally he was sobered by what President McKay said to him next, "That hereafter my life and time would be devoted as a servant of the Lord and that I would hereafter belong to the Church and the whole world."

The next few days would be a blur in the memory of the newest Apostle, the seventy-fourth to serve in the restored Church of Jesus Christ. When he called Claire in Provo he could hardly find his voice to tell her the shocking news. At the Friday afternoon session of the conference, he was so distracted that he left the meeting early to walk aimlessly up to the Utah State Capitol Building. That night he and John attended the Utah-BYU football game during which Howard seemed to focus more upon the fifty-yard line than upon the game.

We are left to speculate about the thoughts which dominated Howard's mind during these stressful hours. It is likely that family was a dominating theme, as with his great-grandfather John Hunter of Paisley, Scotland, whose disaffection from the Church significantly affected Howard's early life and as with his wife, Claire, whose love and caring concern had enabled them to create an ideal Latter-day Saint home of culture and refinement.

President Hunter attended the Saturday morning session of conference in a high state of anticipation. In his own words, he was in panic. As the sustaining of Church officers was conducted by President J. Reuben Clark Jr., his agitation increased. "My heart commenced to pound as I wondered what the reaction would be when my name was read. I have never had such a feeling of panic. One by one the names of the Council of the Twelve were read and my name was the twelfth." If Howard believed the reading of his name would bring relief from the panic which had come upon him, he was mistaken. As he heeded President Clark's invitation and walked to the stand amidst the news photographer's flashbulbs, he said, "My heart increased its pounding as I climbed the steps. Elder Hugh B. Brown moved over to make room for me and I took my place as the twelfth member of the Quorum. I felt the eyes of everyone fastened upon me as well as the weight of the world on my shoulders. As the conference proceeded I was most uncomfortable and wondered if I could ever feel that this was my proper place." The final moment of high excitement to the new Apostle during the conference came at the last session on Sunday afternoon when he was called upon as the concluding speaker. It was an experience which never became easy during his thirty-six years of apostolic service. His words from that pulpit would be recorded to become part of the prophetic literature of the Church. Therefore, he was especially careful about what was said there, realizing that words have meaning and consequences and that his words would be studied and analyzed by the Saints, the scholars, and the scorners over the generations.

His remarks were brief yet comprehensive, combining biography and testimony. His concluding statement set the tone for the thousands of sermons he would deliver during his apostolic ministry. Said he, "President McKay, I want you to know, and all of the membership of the Church to know that I accept without reservation the call which you have made of me, and I am willing to devote my life and all that I have in this service. Sister Hunter joins me in this pledge."

Following the conference, there remained one other signal event necessary to launch Elder Hunter on his apostolic career. This would take place the following Thursday at the weekly meeting of the Council of the First Presidency and Quorum of the Twelve. In the meantime, there were many details to be resolved as he began the process of orientation to his new duties, winding up his professional and business affairs, and arranging for his move to Salt Lake City. This entailed extensive meetings with President David O. McKay and later with President Henry D. Moyle in which he was briefed on his new duties. He also was counseled to retain his residence in California until his professional and business commitments were fulfilled. In the meantime, he would be expected to attend the weekly council meetings in the Salt Lake Temple each Thursday. Between these briefings, Elder Hunter was shown his office in the Administration Building, and arrangements were made for secretarial assistance and for handling his travel and other expenses connected with his Church duties.

Elder Hunter had a preview of the setting where the Council of the First Presidency and Quorum of the Twelve would convene on Thursday, October 15, 1959. It had been given to him by Elder Spencer W. Kimball of the Twelve. The two of them had gone alone to the fourth floor of the Salt Lake Temple where Howard was shown the Upper Room and the adjacent quarters. To see this well-known room for the first time, with its twelve upholstered chairs arranged in a semi-circle facing three identical chairs against the west wall of the room, was an emotional experience for the new member of the Twelve. Here he would meet regularly with his brethren of the Quorum of the Twelve and the First Presidency during the next thirty-six years, moving steadily around the semicircle until time he would occupy the center chair at the west wall.

There was an air of expectancy as the members of the Council assembled in the Upper Room on October 15, 1959. The ceremony to be performed there was of paramount significance to the Church. There Elder Hunter was to become invested with every key and authority necessary for him to preside over The Church of Jesus Christ of Latter-day Saints in its worldwide scope. However, this vast authority was to be latent until two events transpired: that he survive to be the senior living Apostle and that he then be ordained as the President of the Church by the Quorum of the Twelve Apostles. By this means an unbroken chain of apostolic authority is perpetuated in the Church throughout time.

Before all of the assembled Apostles placed their hands upon Elder Howard W. Hunter's head for his ordination, he was given the traditional apostolic charge. It was delivered by President David O. McKay. In it Howard was instructed in the fourfold commitments which inhere in the apostleship: unity, confidentiality, collegiality, and diligence. All the members of his quorum were to be unified before a Church policy, principle, or practice could become effective. Although he was the newest member of the Twelve, his voice would be given equal weight with all the other Apostles. All matters discussed by the Twelve were to be held in strict confidence. Thereafter his life was to be committed to the worldwide work and interests of The Church of Jesus Christ of Latter-day Saints. Following this charge, Elder Hunter accepted it with full heart, adding his fervent testimony to the reality and the divinity of his Savior, Jesus Christ, and his commitment to devote his energies to the work of his quorum through all his days. Thereupon, all of the Apostles laid their hands upon the head of Elder Hunter and, with

President McKay acting as voice, he was ordained an Apostle in the Melchizedek Priesthood of the Church and was set apart as a member of the Quorum of the Twelve Apostles. By these actions Elder Hunter formally and historically became the seventy-fourth person in the history of the restored Church to be ordained an Apostle and inducted into the Quorum of the Twelve Apostles.

A month from his fifty-second birthday, Howard was the youngest member of his quorum, whose average age was sixty-seven. It counted among its membership men of high achievement and character. One of its number, Elder Ezra Taft Benson, lived at the moment in the environs of Washington, D.C., while serving in the cabinet of President Dwight D. Eisenhower. Two others, Elders Harold B. Lee and Marion G. Romney, missed the general conference where Howard was sustained, being away on international assignments.

Following the general conference, Howard was inundated with calls and messages of congratulation. He was amazed by this outpouring of love and support. It was different from the congratulations he had received upon being called as the stake president. People now regarded him in an entirely different light. This position would not, as others had, take only a few years—this was a call for life. He soon learned the truth of what President McKay told him at the time of his call, that as an Apostle he would belong to the Church and to the world. Members of the Church would no longer regard him in quite the same way. He was different. He was special. Indeed, he was a special witness of the divinity of the Lord Jesus Christ. He would be honored the remainder of his life because of the new apostolic mantle he bore.

When Howard and Claire arrived at the Los Angeles airport following general conference, he was met by those to whom his call meant more than to anyone else: his parents, his sister, Dorothy, and her daughters Susan and Kathy. Also with them was Howard's longtime friend and counselor in the stake presidency, J. Talmage Jones. These dear ones would bask in the reflected glow of Howard's call the remainder of their lives. Especially was this true of his parents, Will and Nellie Hunter. His call, in a sense, was a validation of their parental role in his life. They could be justifiably proud of helping to shape his early years.

Back home in California, Elder Hunter began a regimen he would follow until he and Claire moved to Salt Lake City. He would work in his Los Angeles office until midweek, when he would travel to Salt Lake by train or airplane. After attending the weekly meeting of the Council of the First Presidency and Quorum of the Twelve on Thursday, he would return home by the same means. Soon he was assigned to preside at stake conferences on weekends where he would instruct local leaders and congregations and occasionally would reorganize stake presidencies. He also continued to serve as the president of the Pasadena Stake until the last week in November, although he delegated most of his stake responsibilities to his counselors.

President Joseph Fielding Smith presided at the reorganization of the Pasadena Stake, assisted by Elder Hunter. The event produced a nostalgic response in his record: "This has been the most enjoyable experience of my life. I have loved the work and the people I have worked with. I was called to serve as stake president on February 27, 1950, and this is the 40th quarterly conference I have conducted. . . . People were very kind to me afterward, and as I went to my office to get my hat, I had a big lump in my throat."

Throughout the process of winding down his affairs in California, Elder Hunter was working intermittently with his law partner, Gordon Lund, to close out his legal commitments and responsibilities. He completed this process on July 2, 1960, when he made another nostalgic entry in his personal record: "Today I finished most of my work at the office. Nearly all of the pending matters are completed. I was alone in the office today with the realization that my practice of law was now at an end, I made notes on a number of files and left them on the desk for Gordon. I had a sick feeling as I left the office. I have enjoyed the practice of law and it has been my life for the last number of years, but in spite of this, I am pleased and happy to respond to the great call which has come to me in the Church."

Two days later, Howard and Claire departed for the Pacific where they were to meet Richard at the conclusion of his mission in Australia. This was something they had planned for months before Howard's call to the Twelve. Because Richard's release had come such a relatively short time after his call, Elder Hunter was reluctant at first to go forward with their plans. However, when he discussed the matter with the prophet, President McKay urged him to go forward with his plans to travel to meet Richard and then around the world. However, Elder Hunter was given Church assignments to fill during the course of his travels. So, before joining Richard, he presided at district conferences in Japan, Taiwan, and Hong Kong.

After his release in Australia, Richard flew to join his parents in Hong Kong. They then followed generally the travel plan Howard and Claire had followed with John. Along the way, Elder Hunter conducted other Church meetings in such places as Saigon, Vietnam, where he met with servicemen, organizing a Church group among them. Their tour was a joyous experience for the Hunters and their youngest son, who had completed an honorable mission. The only incident which marred the otherwise delightful experience occurred in Calcutta, India, where Claire fell and broke her wrist.

In February 1961, the Hunters sold their home in California. Because Howard had closed out his legal affairs, it was time to move to Salt Lake City. They had purchased a lot in the Oak Hills subdivision on the east bench and planned to build a new home there. During the period of construction, they first rented the home of Bryan Bunker, president of the California Mission, then for several months after President Bunker returned, they rented an apartment on Capitol Hill in Salt Lake City, a few blocks north of Howard's office in the Church Administration Building. On July 22, 1963, the Hunters moved into their new home, the first one which had been built to their specifications. Claire had spent many hours selecting the furniture and fixtures for their home, which included choice glassware, artwork, and original sculptures.

Throughout this period of relocation which had stretched into almost four years, Elder Hunter had pursued his apostolic duties with vigor. He was becoming well-known to the members of the Church, having spoken at eight general conferences since his introduction into the Twelve. He also spoke on the nationwide "Church of the Air" broadcast on Sunday morning preceding the Tabernacle Choir broadcast during the April 1960 general conference. Meanwhile, Elder Hunter was inducted into the behind-the-scenes activities of a General Authority when, over a period of months, he was assigned to serve on the general priesthood committee, the general welfare committee, the missionary committee, the Church personnel committee, and the BYU Board of Trustees, among other assignments.

On November 17, 1960, Elder Hunter received a sensitive assignment which would bring him into close association with the First Presidency. On that day he was called to review and to make recommendations about requests to the First Presidency from divorced persons who sought permission to receive temple recommends. This entailed reviewing documentation as to the reasons for the divorce, together with reports and recommendations from local leaders. After reviewing the record, Elder Hunter would make a recommendation to the First Presidency who would then decide. Elder Hunter was selected for this confidential assignment because of his background as an attorney and counselor. It was an assignment which previously had been filled by President J. Reuben Clark Jr. Later, Elder Hunter's duties were expanded to include requests for the cancellation of temple sealings. Elder Hunter filled this sensitive role until February 1970, a period of almost ten years. During that time, he reviewed thousands of these cases. Each one received his careful and precise scrutiny. Sometimes the recommendations he made were heart-wrenching, given the traumatic background which had given rise to a request. In the later years of his service in this assignment, the First Presidency approved Elder Hunter's recommendation that stake presidents be authorized to decide the cases of requests for divorce clearance. These and many other ad hoc assignments kept Elder Hunter heavily involved during the periods he spent at home.

December 8, 1961, was another red-letter day for the Hunter family. On that day Elder Hunter performed the temple sealing for his son Richard and Nan Greene. During this period of time, Elder Hunter also spent time conducting research about the Middle East. This was in preparation for a trip he and Elder Spencer W. Kimball had planned to the Holy Land. The two Apostles and their wives, Camilla Kimball and Claire Hunter, departed from Salt Lake City in mid-December 1961. They would be gone for six weeks. Near the end of their travels in the Holy Land, the two Apostles collaborated in sending a report to their brethren of the Twelve: "This was a glorious experience," they wrote. "We traveled literally from Dan to Beersheba, from the trans-Jordan to the Mediterranean. . . . We lived again the history of the Middle East, secular and ecclesiastical. We believe these travels will have made us more aware of the realness of the past; the relationship of the past to the present; and our debt to our Lord whose life and death seem ever more real."

At Istanbul the Apostles separated in order to fill assignments given to them by President Joseph Fielding Smith. The Kimballs traveled to Germany and the Netherlands while the Hunters went to Switzerland and England, where they held meetings in seven different missions. The two couples met again in Berlin after the Apostles had completed their assignments. Before departing for home from Berlin, the couples visited the Berlin Wall in East Berlin. "Soldiers were patrolling both sides of the wall," wrote Elder Hunter. "Although I have read about the tyranny of communism, I had never before realized what freedom really means. My heart goes out to those who live under the tension of constant fear."

A special rapport existed between Elder Hunter and Elder Kimball, which was enhanced by their lengthy tour through the Holy Land. A leader of the Church in Samoa once commented on this affinity: "Elder Hunter has a special way with the Polynesian people, and is particularly sensitive to cultural differences. In that respect he is like President Kimball."

During his apostolic service Elder Hunter had many opportunities to serve among the Polynesian Saints. In 1968, he and Elder Thomas S. Monson created the Nuku'alofa Stake in Tonga. The two Apostles were struck by the cordiality and the enthusiasm with which they were welcomed. "As we went down the reception line the band played and the crowd gathered to shake hands with us and put leis around our necks. We have never been welcomed by such a crowd." Later the Apostles were granted an interview with the king of Tonga, Taufa'ahau Tupou IV, a "very large man," reputed to weigh over four hundred pounds. Ushered into the royal reception room, they found the monarch seated upon a sofa at the end of the room who greeted them with regal dignity. They found the king to be "a very pleasant and cordial man," who graciously accepted the best wishes of President David O. McKay extended by the Apostles. The feelings of amity created by this apostolic embassy, and others which followed, inured to the benefit of the Church in its proselytizing among the Tongan people and in other ways, including the contribution Tongan players have made to the prowess of the Brigham Young University football teams.

On another visit to the South Pacific, Elder Hunter was presented with a tabua in Fiji, "the highest honor that can be paid to a king or a visiting dignitary." The tabua is a whale's tooth encased in braided fabric. The Fijians attach such significance to the tabua that one cannot be removed from the islands without special permission. Elder Hunter later received such permission in a letter from the Secretary of Fijian Affairs.

While in Samoa in 1974 to organize the Upolu Samoa South Stake, Elder Hunter was treated to the spectacle of an ancient Samoan ceremony. Present were most of the high chiefs from the southern part of the island. Following eloquent speeches by the talking chiefs and amid "the pomp and splendor of the ancient ceremony," Elder Hunter and other visiting dignitaries were served the kava, a specially prepared ceremonial nectar, given to them by the royal cupbearer. Then an elaborate procession followed to display the gifts exchanged by the chiefs, which included twenty-five fine woven mats, roast pigs, a cow, baskets, and beads.

Like others of his brethren in the Quorum, Elder Hunter found that babies in different parts of the world were named after him. One of the most unusual of these was a baby son born to the president of the Tonga Nuku'alofa Mission, Pita F. Hopoate. The name given to the infant was Howard Hunter-i-apai Hopoate—H. H. H. for short. Because the letter H in Tongan is pronounced "Ha," Elder Hunter was amused that his namesake's nickname was pronounced "Ha Ha Ha."

CHAPTER TEN

VARIETY IN APOSTOLIC SERVICE

During his apostolic career, Elder Hunter served in a number of executive positions which, strictly speaking, were not ecclesiastical in nature. He brought to these the same dedication and creativity shown in the roles wherein he directly exercised priesthood authority.

Polynesian Cultural Center

Elder Hunter's extensive involvement with the Saints in the islands of the Pacific and his natural rapport with them brought an unexpected assignment. It was outlined in a letter to him dated January 13, 1965, from the First Presidency. In it he was appointed as the president and chairman of the board of the Polynesian Cultural Center at Laie, Hawaii. The center, which was located adjacent to the Church College of Hawaii, had been opened in

October 1963 as a means of showcasing the talents and the cultural heritage of the students attending the college, students from the islands of Hawaii, Tonga, Samoa, Fiji, Tahiti, and New Zealand. From the time of its creation until the appointment of Elder Hunter, the PCC had been managed by a twenty-seven–member board of directors, which included stake and mission presidents and representatives of the Polynesian students. With a smaller board and with broad executive authority given to him, Elder Hunter was able to move forward and develop the center as a profitable enterprise which also became a significant instrument in advancing the ecclesiastical interests of the Church.

One of the core objectives of the PCC was to provide employment for students at the college, whose wages helped pay tuition and living costs. The financial engine which produced these wages was driven by two activities: first, the sale of Polynesian handicrafts produced at the six villages which comprised the center; second, proceeds generated by performances at a theater where Polynesian students dramatized their cultural heritage through dance and song amid colorful costumes and pageantry. The proceeds from such performances were augmented by funds from elaborate feasts featuring Polynesian food.

When Elder Hunter became the CEO of the cultural center, the dinner theater seated 750. Later the seating capacity was increased to 1,400 and later still to 2,500. This growth was fueled both by word of mouth and by a deliberate strategy of Elder Hunter to publicize the center through the mass media. Relying, no doubt, on his many experiences with programs staged there, Elder Hunter was instrumental in booking the PCC shows at the Hollywood Bowl in Los Angeles for four nights of performances. Afterward the music critic of the *Los Angeles Times* exulted: "In the fifty years of its history, it is unlikely that the Hollywood Bowl has ever been the scene of a more uniquely beautiful spectacle than 'Festival Polynesia.'" Later, the center reached a national audience when segments of the show were televised on *The Ed Sullivan Show*.

Aside from his executive responsibility to formulate, guide, and expand the creative and business path of the PCC, Elder Hunter had to insure that those for whom it had been created, the students, understood its purpose and their role in it. Thus, following a meeting with the students at the college, he observed: "Several of us spoke and reviewed the purposes and objectives of the Cultural Center in helping students receive an education which would otherwise be impossible."

Progress in developing the PCC was slow at first. During the third year of his service as the CEO and chairman of the board, Elder Hunter reported the status of the center: "We are now in the third year of operation. Loss for the first year amounted to over $600,000, for the last year about $70,000. This year we hope to bring it to the break-even point. . . . Even though the loss was $70,000 last year, we paid the sum of $150,000 to apply on students' tuition."

Elder Hunter continued to serve as the CEO and chairman of the board until April 1976 when he was replaced by Elder Marvin J. Ashton of the Twelve. At the time, Elder Hunter reviewed his service in this challenging assignment: "This brings to a close the period of twelve years I have headed this enterprise. During that time we have converted from a substantial operating loss to a very profitable operation. Thousands of students from the South Pacific have been assisted in getting their education, most of whom would not have been able to leave their islands to go to school except for this assistance. The center has given large sums to the BYU–Hawaii campus, has been a major factor in building the image of the Church and promoting a missionary effort, has improved the community of Laie and has become the most patronized tourist attraction in Hawaii. It is a viable unit of the Church, and I have enjoyed the assignment given me by the First Presidency to make it successful."

In his efforts directing the PCC, whereby Laie had become a major tourist attraction in Hawaii, Elder Hunter had played a key role in fulfilling a startling prophecy of President David O. McKay. In February 1955 during groundbreaking ceremonies for the Church College of Hawaii, later to become BYU–Hawaii, the prophet declared that Laie was destined to become "a missionary factor, influencing not thousands, not tens of thousands, but millions of people who will come seeking to know what this town and its significance are." The boldness and the accuracy of this prophecy become apparent when one considers the inconsequential status of Laie when it was uttered. It was a remote village on the north shore of Oahu set in the midst of a bucolic landscape. Few people visited it from the outside, except for Latter-day Saints who came to attend the holy temple, the only building of note in the area. There was nothing else to attract people to Laie. Indeed, at that day Hawaii itself had not become the tourist mecca it later became. The magnet which drew people to Laie in the millions was the sense that the culture and tradition of the South Pacific islands had become concentrated in one place for people from everywhere to see and enjoy. More than that, there was the nightly performance of colorful dance and song accompanied by a sumptuous Polynesian feast. It was a must for the Hawaii vacationer.

Elder Hunter's service at the PCC was reflective of his entire apostolic ministry. He did not seek the position; neither did he shrink from it. He served diligently, creatively, and almost anonymously.

He never sought the spotlight or the headline. The advances made by the PCC during his tenure were phenomenal measured by any standard. No one would ever infer that from his brief summary of his service. He had come, he had served, and he had left for other assignments.

The Genealogical Society

During part of his tenure as the CEO of the PCC, Elder Hunter also served as the president of the Genealogical Society. He was called to this position on January 21, 1964. Because of this calling, he also became a member of the All-Church Coordinating Committee, an organization which knit together the missionary, welfare, home teaching, and genealogy work of the priesthood. This placed him at the very heart of the seismic changes in Church organization and procedure effected by the adoption of the correlation program in the Church. In that position he was able to direct the Genealogical Department in a way consistent with the overall plan while giving his input toward strengthening and perfecting it.

A major challenge facing Elder Hunter at the threshold of this assignment was to bring the department into the modern age of computer technology. This process had been started by his predecessor, N. Eldon Tanner, who had been called as a Counselor in the First Presidency in October 1963. From the time of its creation, the Genealogical Society had relied upon labor-intensive, time-consuming practices in preparing names for use in vicarious temple ordinances. Computer technology offered a means of accelerating that process while increasing its accuracy. Because he would preside over this transformation, Elder Hunter decided he would have to acquire a level of computer competence. To that end, he enrolled in a computer seminar sponsored by IBM in San Jose, California.

During a week of intensive training, he acquired basic knowledge about computers which enabled him to understand the concepts and the technical language as he gave direction to converting the Church's records from paper to a computer database. This required time and patience. The conversion was essentially completed by the time of his release as president of the Genealogical Society on May 7, 1972.

Meanwhile, Elder Hunter pressed forward with another project which had been started by his predecessor. This was the Granite Mountain Vault near the mouth of Little Cottonwood Canyon on the east bench of the Salt Lake Valley. Here cavernous tunnels had been carved into the granite mountain which would serve as a secure repository where vital Church records could be protected indefinitely from physical hazards. The project was completed in June 1966 when on the twenty-second of that month it was formally dedicated at a gathering in one of the huge storage rooms of the vault. Present were many of the General Authorities, Church employees, and special guests. Elder Hunter conducted the service while President Hugh B. Brown offered the dedicatory prayer.

In consultation with Elder Theodore M. Burton, Assistant to the Twelve, Brother George H. Fudge, a longtime employee of the department, and others, Elder Hunter conducted a detailed study and analysis of the department. This resulted in converting the library to open stacks which facilitated the finding and use of materials. The society discontinued doing research for patrons, instead referring them to professional genealogists. Branch libraries were established in numerous stake centers outside Salt Lake City. A pedigree referral service was established which brought together researchers working on the same surnames. In addition, recommendations were made to the First Presidency and approved by them for in internal procedures. These changes created more flex- in the sequence of performing vicarious ordinances. These and other changes increased the efficiency and the serviceability of the department.

His experience in staging events in the Hollywood Bowl and in publicizing the Polynesian Cultural Center had shown Elder Hunter how such public events helped validate an organization in the public mind. For this and other reasons, he undertook to commemorate the organization of the Genealogical Society by holding the first World Conference on Records. This groundbreaking event was joined with a World Conference and Seminar on Genealogy. The gathering convened in the newly constructed Salt Palace in downtown Salt Lake City. The event attracted more than 6,000 delegates from around the world. Elder Hunter welcomed the delegates and addressed them, emphasizing "our collective responsibility to preserve the records of the world." In assessing the value of the conference, Elder Hunter observed, "Although this has been a tremendous undertaking and has consumed months of hard work, we feel it has resulted in enhancing our position as the dominant organization in genealogy in the world."

Later, Elder Hunter represented the Church at the International Congress on Archives held in Moscow and the Tenth International Congress of Genealogical and Heraldic Sciences in Vienna. In 1971, Elder Hunter led the negotiations to obtain permission to microfilm records in Italy. These and other initiatives prompted the comment from him, "Doors are being opened to us in many countries where we were previously barred from the records."

Church Historian

Elder Hunter served as Church Historian for less than two years, January 25, 1970, until January 13, 1972. But this short time was filled with events of historic importance to the Church. His call came on January 25, only a few days following the death of President David O. McKay. During that interval, Elder Hunter witnessed one of the most intriguing scenes in the Church: the installation of a new prophet, seer, and revelator. It was a drama in which he participated actively as a member of the Twelve.

At the moment of President McKay's death, Joseph Fielding Smith, the President of the Twelve and the senior living Apostle in terms of service, instantly became the de facto President of the Church. Six days later in the Upper Room of the Salt Lake Temple, that status as the President of the Church was ratified and affirmed when Elder Hunter and all the other members of the Twelve placed their hands upon his head and, with Elder Harold B. Lee acting as voice, President Joseph Fielding Smith was ordained and set apart as the tenth President of The Church of Jesus Christ of Latter-day Saints. The simplicity of the act obscured its vast significance. Without debate, campaigning, or controversy the ultimate earthly authority over a worldwide Church, its members, officers, and possessions had thus become vested in a ninety-four-year-old man. To one like Elder Hunter, trained in the law under a democratic system, this was extraordinary, for President Smith alone possessed the ultimate earthly executive, legislative, and judicial authority over the entire Church.

The office of Church Historian and Recorder to which Elder Hunter was called is one mandated by revelation. "It is the duty of the Lord's clerk . . . to keep a history, and a general church record of all things that transpire in Zion" (D&C 85:1). He was the seventeenth man to occupy this position. His immediate predecessor was President Joseph Fielding Smith, who had held the position for forty-nine years. The stature of President Smith and the other Church Historians, the magnitude of the responsibilities, and the surprise of the call filled Elder Hunter with a sense of inadequacy: "I was taken so completely by surprise that I didn't at the moment feel the impact of the awesome responsibility of this assignment. President Smith had been the Church Historian for so many years that I could hardly visualize myself in that position. The assignment as given by the Lord through revelation is tremendously challenging—both in fulfilling the task of collecting and writing and in making the material of use to the members of the Church" (*Improvement Era*, April 1970, 26). This call also placed Elder Hunter in charge of the Church Library Coordinating Committee and the Church's record management program. In these positions he was assisted by a staff of forty-eight in overseeing more than 260,000 bound volumes and almost a million pamphlets, photos, recordings, and documents.

Characteristically, Elder Hunter immediately began to assess the scope of his new responsibilities and to devise a plan for fulfilling them. He began by consulting with members of his staff whose knowledge of the department extended over many years. He also sought counsel from professionals outside the department whose knowledge and experience about managing and preserving large archives would prove helpful. This included a conducted tour of the massive library and archive at Harvard University. Meanwhile, Elder Hunter dipped into some of the sensitive and sacred documents in the Historical Department archive which shed inspiring light upon events surrounding the origins of the Church. These [illegible]ed with Elder Hunter who wrote: "I too have had a deep interest in history. I have a 20-volume work containing the history of civilizations, which I have enjoyed reading and rereading. I believe that when we understand what has gone on in the past we can make better plans for the future." During this period there were many discussions among the First Presidency and the Twelve about relieving members of the Twelve of principal administrative assignments at Church headquarters in order to free them up for their apostolic responsibility of promulgating the gospel and setting in order the affairs of the Church around the world. From this it could be easily inferred that Elder Hunter's tenure as the Church Historian would be short-lived.

During this period Elder Hunter was invited to participate in an event of major historical significance for the Church. This was the first area general conference to be held in Manchester, England, on August 27–29, 1971. President Joseph Fielding Smith and his First Counselor, President Harold B. Lee, led seven members of the Twelve to England for this conference. In addition to Elder Hunter, these included: Acting President of the Twelve, Spencer W. Kimball, and Elders Marion G. Romney, Richard L. Evans, Gordon B. Hinckley, Thomas S. Monson, and Boyd K. Packer. This gathering was the first of a series of area general conferences held around the world designed to emphasize the international character of the Church and to encourage members of the Church to remain in their home countries rather than to immigrate to America.

Assembled in Manchester were some 15,000 members of the Church from various parts of Great Britain. Meetings were held in the Belle Vue Center, with the general sessions being held in Kings Hall. The building had been altered to simulate, as much as was possible, the Tabernacle in Salt Lake City. Special upholstered chairs were made for the General Authorities and carpeting placed on the special temporary stand. Sound technicians were sent to England from the United States to check out and adjust the sound system.

In the evening before the conference began, the members of the First Presidency and the Quorum of the Twelve gathered in a conference room of the Piccadilly Hotel. Because eight members of the Council of the First Presidency and Quorum of the Twelve were present, this constituted an official meeting of the Council, the first one ever held outside the boundaries of the United States. An official meeting of the Twelve had been held at Carpenters Hall in Manchester in 1840, but no members of the First Presidency were present.

As the incumbent Church Historian, Elder Hunter was in his element, finding himself in an environment where so many important events in the early history of the Church in the British Isles had unfolded. Of special import were remarks made by President Spencer W. Kimball and Elder Marion G. Romney. President Kimball had with him a transcript of the diary his grandfather, Heber C. Kimball, had kept when he led the first group of Mormon missionaries to proselytize in England. President Kimball referred to an entry in that diary which recorded an incident when his grandfather was so emotionally affected one day that he twice had to go to a nearby stream to wash the tears from his eyes. President Kimball said his grandfather later discussed this incident with the Prophet Joseph Smith, who told him he was affected this way because he was in an area which had been visited by the Savior following His Resurrection. In his remarks, Elder Romney alluded to the conversion of his ancestor, Miles Romney, who, with his wife, was converted as the result of a street meeting held by Heber C. Kimball's missionaries in nearby Preston, England. Elder Romney noted parenthetically that from those conversions had sprung a Romney progeny of several thousand members of the Church.

Elder Hunter delivered two sermons during this area conference. Both were models of precise eloquence. Both treated subjects of prime importance. The first, delivered at the priesthood session, emphasized the importance of working in the London Temple: "Several things are accomplished by our attendance at the temple—we comply with the instructions of the Lord to accomplish our own ordinance work, we bless our families by the sealing ordinances, and we share our blessings with others by doing for them what they cannot do for themselves. In addition to these, we lift our own thoughts, grow closer to the Lord, honor our priesthood and spiritualize our lives" (First British area general conference report, 100). The second, delivered at the concluding general session, focused on the last of the Lord's parables, "the parable of the entrusted talents or capabilities." Elder Hunter said, "Talents are not given to us to be put on display or to be hidden away but to be used. The Master expects us to make use of them. He expects us to venture forth and increase what we have been given according to our capacities and abilities" (Ibid., 172). The effect of these words is greater today than when they were uttered because we can witness how they affected the life of the speaker.

This first area general conference had an enormous positive effect upon the Latter-day Saints in the British Isles. This was illustrated following the concluding general session of the conference. The prophet and his traveling companions had to leave immediately following the meeting in order to catch a flight. As they departed, the entire audience stood in silent respect until they had left the arena. Then without prompting, someone began to sing "We Thank Thee, O God, for a Prophet" (*Hymns*, no. 19). Soon everyone joined in to sing all of the verses. Afterward no one spoke, and there was no movement toward the exits. Then a voice was heard singing "God Be with You Till We Meet Again" (*Hymns*, no. 152). Once more the audience picked it up to sing all the verses. Silence followed with no movement to leave. Then something unheard of in a Latter-day Saint gathering occurred—the audience began to applaud, everyone joining in an enthusiastic yet respectful show of appreciation for the conference. Even then there was little movement toward the exits, the audience showing little inclination to end what to them had been a joyous, uplifting experience. Most of those present had come from small, isolated congregations who were amazed and heartened to see 15,000 British Latter-day Saints in one gathering. In token that the British Saints had understood and had taken to heart the purpose of the conference, the choir sang an original composition during the last session titled "This Is Our Place." The concluding verse tells the story:

> *This is our place; here we will stay,*
> *To build and strengthen Ward and Stake,*
> *Until the Lord supreme shall reign,*
> *This is our place; here we will serve.*

When Elder Hunter returned to Salt Lake City following the Manchester conference, he found that discussions about relieving members of the Twelve of major administrative responsibilities at Church headquarters were moving forward rapidly. These came to fruition in January 1972. At that time the historical department was restructured to provide for a managing director of the department with a Church historian and a Church archivist serving under him. Elder Alvin R. Dyer and Brothers Leonard J. Arrington and Earl L.

Olsen were appointed to these positions, respectively. Elder Hunter retained oversight responsibility for the department.

BYU New World Archeological Foundation

Despite his release as Church Historian in 1972, Elder Hunter continued to fill a role of leadership connected with ancient history. In January 1961, he had been appointed chairman of the board of the BYU New World Archeological Foundation. He served in this position for twenty-four years. The foundation was a professional research organization based at Brigham Young University. Its purpose was to study archeological sites in southern Mexico and northern Central America to ascertain possible connections with sites referred to in the Book of Mormon. Elder Hunter was not content with the supervisory aspects of this assignment but insisted on participating in as many field trips as his busy schedule allowed. As a result his records are peppered with accounts of his forays into remote areas to inspect ancient archeological sites. Often he combined these trips with assignments to tour missions or attend stake conferences.

An account of a visit to El Mirador in Guatemala provides a realistic flavor of what he encountered: "They took us to some of the excavations and to the top of El Tigre, one of the highest of the temple mounds. On the way back we watched hundreds of spider monkeys swinging through the tops of the trees. The parrots and toucans were screeching and the whole jungle seemed to be alive. We kept a lookout for snakes. The rains earlier in the month have driven them into the trees and several workers on archeological sites have died from their bites. We saw three snakes on the trail. One was the deadly bushmaster, one a coral, and the other we couldn't identify. About four o'clock the howler monkeys came, yelping and howling in the trees. . . . We had dinner in the mess tent—rice and beans. Brother Bradford [Elder William P. Bradford of the Seventy] and I slept on top of sleeping bags in a tent with net siding to keep out the mosquitoes and bugs."

Elder Hunter's numerous visits to these remote sites deep in the jungle, made over a period of almost a quarter of a century, always reminded him of the text of the Book of Mormon. He knew that the findings of the foundation, regardless of their appeal, could never prove the truthfulness of the Book of Mormon. A personal witness of the book could be obtained only by spiritual means, the same means by which he acquired a witness and testimony of the reality and the divinity of the Lord Jesus Christ. "It is by the power of the Holy Ghost that I bear my witness," he said. "I know of Christ's reality as if I had seen with my eyes and heard with my ears" ("An Apostle's Witness of Christ," *Ensign*, January 1984, 70). So it was with Elder Hunter's witness of the Book of Mormon. He was heard to say, "Joseph Smith did not write that book. He lacked the knowledge and the experience to do so."

Elder Hunter's visit to a Mayan archeological site in November 1975 capped one of the most extraordinary sequences of apostolic service ever. Earlier that month he had completed a restructuring of the five stakes in Mexico City, creating fifteen stakes out of the five. Assisted by Elder J. Thomas Fyans, this entailed reordering the boundary lines for all of the new stakes, interviewing dozens of local leaders, then selecting from this pool and calling, setting apart, and instructing fifteen new stake presidencies. In addition, this involved the calling of new bishops to replace those who had been called into stake presidencies. This was intensive and demanding work which continued late into the night, taxing the spiritual insights and perceptions of Elder Hunter and his assistant. He later explained the reasons for this unprecedented action: "Our purpose was to reduce the size of the stakes, to better align them, to reduce travel of members, and also to provide for the rapid growth that is taking place in Mexico." He also noted that "smaller stakes can be better trained, that leadership can be more effective and the anticipated growth of about 1,000 members commencing in March will be better fellowshipped." As a postscript to that frenetic weekend, it should be noted that in the interval between it and the visit to the Mayan archeological site, he and Elder Fyans held a three-day seminar with mission presidents serving in southern Mexico and Central America and organized the Poza Rica Mexico Stake, carved from the Mexico Vera Cruz Mission. Then, on his way home from Mexico, he stopped in Houston, Texas, to reorganize the Houston Texas Stake. On returning to Salt Lake City he observed, "We were tired by the time we got home."

Elder Hunter's work in restructuring the stakes in Mexico City became a cause célèbre among his brethren and the source of good-natured banter between them. The following year when he reported creating three new stakes in Mexico, President Spencer W. Kimball wondered about the cause of his diminished performance. And later, when Elder Bruce R. McConkie reported creating five stakes in South America, his brethren, with tongues in cheek, chided him for trying to exceed Elder Hunter's record.

As a postscript to Elder Hunter's role in restructuring stakes, consider this: When the presidents of three stakes on the east bench of Salt Lake City submitted a request to restructure their stakes' boundaries, the matter was referred to Elder Hunter to handle. I was the president of one of the stakes and was present when Elder Hunter made his report. He said, in substance, that it was the first time in his experience that he had seen three stake presidents in complete agreement, and therefore he approved the request.

Apostolic Service in the Middle East

Taking into account his two trips around the world with his family, his lengthy tour of the Holy Land with his wife and President and Sister Kimball, and other visits he had made to the area, Elder Hunter was perhaps more conversant with affairs in the Middle East than any other member of the Quorum of the Twelve. It comes as no surprise then that he became deeply involved in two of the most important and historically significant events affecting the Church to take place there during his apostolic ministry. These were the building of the Orson Hyde Memorial Monument and of the BYU Jerusalem Center on the Mount of Olives. By reason of his legal background, his historical knowledge, his personal acquaintance with the area, and his love for the two dominant cultures there, the Israelis and the Palestinians, he was peculiarly equipped to deal with the complex and emotionally charged issues faced in bringing these two projects to fruition. In reviewing the background of these projects and Elder Hunter's role in them, it is easy to conclude that he was prepared and raised up for the task.

The purpose of the Orson Hyde Monument on the Mount of Olives was to commemorate an apostolic prayer Elder Hyde offered there on October 24, 1841. This historic event was in fulfillment of a mission call he received at the April general conference held in Nauvoo in 1840. Elder John E. Page was called at the same time to accompany Elder Hyde but was unable to fulfill his mission (Jensen, *LDS Biographical Encyclopedia,* 1:81). Elder Hyde traveled first to England, then to Bavaria, then to Alexandria, Egypt, and finally to Jerusalem. "On Sunday morning, October 24, [1841]," he later reported, "a good while before day, I arose from sleep, and went out of the city as soon as the gates were opened, crossed the brook Kedron, and went upon the Mount of Olives, and there, in solemn silence, with pen, ink, and paper, just as I saw in the vision, offered up the following prayer to Him who lives forever and ever" (*History of the Church*, 4:456). In his prayer Elder Hyde pleaded for the return of the Jews to their homeland: "Incline them to gather in upon this land according to Thy word," he pleaded. "Let them come like clouds and like doves to their windows. Let the large ships of the nations bring them from the distant isles; and let kings become their nursing fathers, and queens with motherly fondness wipe the tear of sorrow from their eye" (Ibid., 4:457). Because of the historic significance of this apostolic prayer and its special relevance to the restored Church's message of the gatherings in the latter days, the Church had long hoped that Elder Hyde's prayer, in its entirety, could be placed upon the Mount of Olives in an appropriate setting.

The first positive step toward fulfilling this hope took place in mid-September 1972. At that time the prophet, Harold B. Lee, who two months before had been ordained as the eleventh President of the Church, arrived at Tel Aviv in company with Elder Gordon B. Hinckley of the Twelve and Edwin Q. Cannon, president of the Swiss Mission, which had jurisdiction over the Middle East. The three travelers and their wives were met at the airport by an Israeli official, Mr. Lourie, an assistant to the Israeli Foreign Minister, Abba Eban, who was then in New York. However, in token of his regret at not being able to greet President Lee in person, Mr. Eban left a copy of the book My *People* inscribed to President Lee. Later in the day the prophet met with Dr. Calbi, the Minister of Religion, and with Jerusalem's mayor, Teddy Kollek, to discuss the possibility of constructing a monument on the Mount of Olives commemorating the Orson Hyde story. The prophet was upbeat about the prospects for the monument following these meetings.

Less than three weeks after returning from Jerusalem, President Harold B. Lee was confirmed as the eleventh President of the Church in a solemn assembly held in connection with the October 1972 general conference. Two months later, on December 19, 1972, Elder Hunter received an appointment which would involve him for seven years in complicated transactions which would result in the dedication of the Orson Hyde Memorial Garden on the Mount of Olives. On that December day, President Lee invited Elder Hunter to a meeting of the First Presidency where he was appointed to study the possibility of such a monument during a planned trip to the Holy Land over the holidays. During his stay in Jerusalem on this occasion, Elder Hunter examined several potential sites for the Hyde monument, later reporting his findings and recommendations to President Lee.

The project lay dormant for two years; in the interval, President Lee died unexpectedly in December 1973. The following year, the city of Jerusalem invited the Church to participate in a greenbelt park development surrounding the city, with the Orson Hyde monument to be the largest part of the development. In accepting this invitation, the Church became obligated to contribute a million dollars for the project. To this end, the Orson Hyde Foundation was organized with President N. Eldon Tanner, Elders LeGrand Richards and Howard W. Hunter, and five great-grandchildren of Orson Hyde as the incorporators. Elder Richards became the president and trustee of the foundation, its chief responsibility being to spearhead the fundraising drive which resulted in some 30,000 donors contributing a total of more than one million dollars to the foundation. Meanwhile, the task of negotiating the contracts with the city of Jerusalem and overseeing the actual design and construction of the monument fell chiefly to Elder Hunter. Over a period of five years, he traveled intermittently to Jerusalem to oversee the work on the monument. By October 1979 it was ready for dedication, "an amphitheater in a grottolike setting providing seating for visitors with a view of the Old City and numerous landmarks of Jerusalem. A heroic-size plaque in the garden inscribed in English and Hebrew contains excerpts of Elder Hyde's prayer. The plaque is accessible by winding pathways through groves of trees, plants, and other shrubbery" ("News of the Church," *Ensign*, December 1979, 67–68).

One thousand Latter-day Saints were present in Jerusalem for the dedication, including seven General Authorities. Elder Hunter conducted the service at the monument. Mayor Teddy Kollek presented a medal from the City of Jerusalem to President Kimball and Elders Richards and Hunter. In his remarks, offered before President Kimball dedicated the monument, the mayor expressed gratitude that so many Latter-day Saints had made the effort to come "to the other Jerusalem," an allusion to the Latter-day Saint teaching that a "new Jerusalem" would be built on the American continent. The mayor then said, "Everybody who knows about the history of Jerusalem in comparatively modern times knows about the prophecy of Orson Hyde. And here the Jews are back in Jerusalem again" (Baldridge, *Gathering In*, 53–54). The monument, the ceremony, and the words of Mayor Kollek provided an emphatic affirmation of the efficacy of Elder Hyde's prophetic prayer.

Many of the Latter-day Saints present on this occasion had come by cruise ship, part of a BYU excursion. Elder Hunter was among that number. His experiences with the Croonaders and with Claire on their pre-wedding cruise had introduced and converted him to the amenities of leisurely travel by sea. At midnight following the ceremony on the Mount of Olives, he gathered with a group of friends aboard ship for dinner and quiet conversation about the significance of what they had witnessed.

The Jerusalem Center

On February 8, 1979, several months before the Orson Hyde Monument was dedicated, Elder Hunter began a ten-year odyssey which would culminate in the dedication of the BYU Jerusalem Center on the Mount of Olives in May 1989. On that day in 1979, Elder Hunter conferred with representatives of BYU to discuss the possibility of acquiring property on the Mount of Olives and constructing a multipurpose building there. Two months later he recommended to the First Presidency that the Church "purchase land in Jerusalem for the construction of a building for a branch chapel . . . and for housing and classrooms for the BYU Study Abroad program." That recommendation was approved on August 22, 1979, when Elder Hunter, "assisted by representatives of BYU, was authorized to negotiate for the purchase of a two acre tract in Jerusalem to be used to conduct a branch facility and to provide housing for the BYU Study Abroad program and for a visitors center. . . . Joining Elder Hunter to present the matter were Jeffrey Holland, Dallin H. Oaks, Fred Schwendiman, Robert Taylor (who directs BYU's tour program) and David Galbraith (who is the district president in Israel). These facilities, along with the Orson Hyde Memorial Garden, will give the Church a highly visible presence in Jerusalem" (Author's diary, August 23, 1979).

With this authorization, Elder Hunter undertook one of the most sensitive assignments of his apostolic ministry. Here he would be dealing with land which both the Jews and the Arabs claimed.

Perhaps more than any other General Authority, he was aware of and sensitive to this conflict, which he explained to a BYU audience in 1979: "Both the Jews and the Arabs are . . . children of promise, and as a church we do not take sides. We have love for and an interest in each. The purpose of the gospel of Jesus Christ is to bring about love, unity, and brotherhood of the highest order. . . . To our friends of Judah, we say: We are your brethren of the house of Joseph—we feel a close relationship to you. We are messengers of the true covenant and bear a message that God has spoken in this day and time. To our kinsmen of Abraham, we say: We are your brethren—we look upon no nation or nationality as second-class citizens. We invite all men to investigate our message and to receive our fellowship" ("All Are Alike unto God," *Ensign*, June 1979, 72–74). It was this spirit which characterized all of Elder Hunter's actions during the thorny process which led to the completion of the project.

For two years, efforts to obtain land on the Mount of Olives were fruitless. Every lead turned into a dead end. However, a break came in January 1981, when the registration of Brigham Young University in Israel was approved. Four months later the Israel Lands Authority agreed in principle to lease a five-acre tract to BYU for forty-nine years, with an option to extend for an additional forty-nine years. Finalization of the lease was conditioned upon the submission and approval of architectural plans. Once the architectural plans were completed and submitted for approval, they had to run the gauntlet of a host of Israeli officers and agencies. At last, on September 27, 1983, the Jerusalem District Council approved the plans and that afternoon the Church Board of Education approved the official name of the project—The Jerusalem Center for Near Eastern Studies, Brigham Young University. Later, Elder Hunter, accompanied by Elder James E. Faust and BYU president Jeffrey R. Holland, flew to Israel where, on April 2, 1984, the legal documents were signed. The following December the building permit was issued, and construction began the day before Christmas.

The euphoria among the Latter-day Saints created by this event was overshadowed by a deluge of vocal dissent and outrage. Until that time, the drawn-out proceedings between the City of Jerusalem and BYU had not received wide publicity. But the appearance of construction equipment on the Mount of Olives suddenly aroused the Jews, the Arabs, and the Christian communities in Jerusalem. Elder Hunter reported to the First Presidency, "The Jews have a fear that our presence in Jerusalem is a means of proselyting, and the Arabs are concerned because we are building on what they consider to be occupied land." The Arabs contended that if the Jews wanted to be generous to the Mormons, they should grant them land in west Jerusalem, not land they claimed had been expropriated from them. Publicly the Christian churches in Jerusalem opposed the BYU Center only on environmental grounds, but privately regarded it as an outrage. Newspaper articles calling on the Knesset to rescind the agreement stirred up angry protests at the construction site, threatening violence.

As the tension increased, a behind-the-scenes maneuver was mounted which helped to tamp down the furor. With the aid of political allies, 154 members of the U.S. Congress from both parties signed a letter urging the Israelis to allow the completion of the BYU center. The letter noted that Israel's commitment to democracy and plurality was a major motivation for the signatories' longstanding support of Israel. Moreover, they expressed the view that completion of the center would be "a further source of understanding and cooperation between our two countries." Elder Hunter arranged to have a copy of this letter delivered to each of the 120 members of the Knesset. This action, coupled with an opinion of the attorney general of Israel issued at the time concluding there was no legal means of halting the BYU center, finally resolved the issue and the construction went forward to completion. It must be said, however, that the voices of some of the protestors continued to be heard to the very end.

When President Hunter was in Jerusalem in February 1987, Mayor Kollek assured him the final inspections of the center would be completed within a few weeks, thus allowing BYU to occupy the premises. President Hunter received a telegram from David Galbraith on March 8 advising that eighty students of the Kibbutz Ramut Rachel (where BYU Study Abroad students had previously stayed), with their gear and equipment, had occupied the center on that day. Only the formality of signing the lease remained. On May 8, 1988, the Israeli Cabinet authorized the Lands Authority to issue it. Six days later President Hunter flew to Tel Aviv, accompanied by his son John, Elder and Sister Faust, and President and Sister Holland. Due to serious back surgery Elder Hunter had undergone the previous year, he was in a wheelchair at the time.

The culmination of the lengthy process came on May 18, 1988. On that day the lease was signed in the office of the Jerusalem Lands Authority. Yehuda Ziv signed for the city of Jerusalem, President Holland for the university, and President Hunter for the Church. The signing relieved President Hunter of a great burden of care. Uncertainty about the outcome and the unpleasantness of the protests had taken their toll on his peace of mind. All that was behind him finally, and he had a sense of exuberance.

This feeling carried over to the next day when he and President Holland took Mayor Kollek on a personal tour of the new facility.

The spectacular view of the Old City as seen through the windows of the center intrigued the mayor. He was heard to say he wasn't prepared for the magnificence of the center.

The center was officially dedicated a year later in May 1989. On this occasion President Hunter acted in his role as the President of the Quorum of the Twelve Apostles. He had been set apart as the president following the death, in May 1988, of his friend and mentor, President Marion G. Romney. The party traveling to Jerusalem included President Hunter's son Richard; President Thomas S. Monson, Second Counselor in the First Presidency; and Elder Boyd K. Packer of the Twelve. Shortly before leaving Salt Lake City, President Hunter cut his head in a fall in his office, requiring several stitches. The attending physician had suggested that he have them removed by a physician at a hospital in Tel Aviv. To his surprise, Elder Packer came to his hotel room in Tel Aviv to solve the problem. With him was his daughter-in-law, a registered nurse. Speaking in a professional tone, Elder Packer announced that he had a doctoral degree and had come with his assistant to remove the stitches. The deed was done in an aura of good humor.

President Monson, who was the chairman of the board of trustees of BYU, conducted the services dedicating the Jerusalem Center. It was a solemn yet joyous occasion. Present were fifty invited guests whose attention was divided between the speakers at the rostrum and the magnificent view of the Old City seen through the large windows of the center's auditorium. The speakers included Robert Taylor, director of BYU tours to the Holy Land; Fred J. Schwendiman, who directed the construction of the center; President Holland, recently sustained as a member of the First Quorum of Seventy; and Elder Boyd K. Packer. President Hunter was the concluding speaker and offered the dedicatory prayer.

Under other circumstances, President Monson, as a member of the First Presidency and vice-chairman of the BYU board of trustees, would have offered the dedicatory prayer. In this situation, however, he was junior in apostolic seniority to President Hunter, who stood next in line to become the President of the Church.

In his remarks, President Hunter first sketched some of the many challenges faced and the inspirations received in the construction of the center. The beautiful dedicatory prayer he then offered contained this significant excerpt: "This building wherein we are seated has been constructed for the housing of those who love thee and seek to learn of thee and follow in the footsteps of thy Son, our Savior and Redeemer. It is beautiful in every respect, exemplifying the beauty of what it represents. O Father, we thank thee for the privilege of building this house to thee for the benefit and learning of thy sons and daughters."

CHAPTER ELEVEN

THE IMPERIOUS MANDATE

The dedication of the Jerusalem Center marked a crucial watershed in President Hunter's apostolic service. Ahead were the years during which his chief function would be to direct the work of the members of the Quorum of the Twelve Apostles. Behind him were the years during which he had filled important apostolic assignments, received either from the president of his quorum or from the First Presidency. For thirty years he had fulfilled with honor and with notable ability every special assignment given to him by his presiding officers. Thus he could look back with a sense of satisfaction upon his work in Hawaii with the Polynesian Cultural Center; upon the challenging months with the Genealogical Society when he helped to usher the department into the computer age; upon his brief but rewarding service as the Church Historian; upon the many years of service with the archeological group, including numerous field trips to ancient building sites; and upon the demanding and complicated work in seeing both the Orson Hyde Monument and the BYU Jerusalem Center permanently established upon the Mount of Olives. Amid these significant assignments were thousands of other apostolic duties he filled: reorganizing stakes, touring missions, speaking, writing, counseling, and giving loving service to the sad and the forlorn and those caught up in the trauma of misconduct.

From that time forward, President Hunter's apostolic role would be far different. Now instead of taking on heavy assignments as in the past, his would be the role of providing overall leadership and direction to the Twelve, making assignments, overseeing the work of the patriarchs, and filling international assignments as prompted to do so. Perhaps more important than any of these was the intimidating role imposed upon him by Church history, to stand ready at a moment's notice to assume the prophetic leadership of a worldwide church.

The specific, ad hoc, and other duties President Hunter undertook as a member of the Twelve were overshadowed by his preeminent responsibility as a special witness of the Lord Jesus Christ. This was a duty which colored and gave meaning to his daily activities, whatever their form. It was a duty he could never lay down as long as life lasted. It was a duty which separated and distinguished him from all other priesthood officers in the Church. And it was a duty which connected him spiritually to all those who had worn that mantle before him, or who would later wear it.

This apostolic fraternity traced its genesis in the restored Church to events in 1835 when the Quorum of the Twelve Apostles was created in modern times. A year before the Church was organized, Oliver Cowdery and David Whitmer were directed by revelation to "search out the Twelve" (D&C 18:37). That direction was fulfilled in February 1835 when the first members of the Twelve were called and instructed. In remarks given at the time, Oliver Cowdery enunciated the creed for the Latter-day Apostles. He said, "You will see what you never expected to see; you will need the mind of Enoch or Elijah, and the faith of the brother of Jared; you must be prepared to walk by faith, however appalling the prospect to human view; you, and each of you, should feel the force of the imperious mandate, Son, go labor in my vineyard, and cheerfully receive what comes" (*History of the Church*, 2:197).

As President Hunter met regularly with his brethren over the years, the significance and the force of the imperious mandate became ever more apparent in his life. He was bound to his fellow Apostles, whether living or dead, with an immutable bond of love and dedication to the Lord Jesus Christ. These were the special witnesses of His reality, His divinity, His charity, His love, and His grace. President Hunter never failed to acknowledge his love and respect for the Apostles and his sense of awe that he had been found worthy to be counted among their number. His records are rife with expressions of such feelings: "Sitting with this group of my brethren makes me aware of my inadequacies, but always brings a resolution to try harder"; "Times like these make me feel my own insignificance and unworthiness to be allowed such privileges and blessings"; "These meetings are highlights in my life and always leave me with the question as to why I was selected and why I am privileged to sit in this council"; "I left the temple today, as I have on previous occasions, feeling my inadequacies and wondering why I was selected for this association. I always resolve to attempt to do better and strive to be the example of what is expected."

The questioning and self-doubt about his status among the

Apostles suggested in these statements perhaps explain a signal reason why President Hunter was called to the Twelve. They manifest a genuine humility and a desire to improve. They are devoid of pride and self-seeking. They show complete submissiveness to the demands of his calling, qualities expected in a special witness.

As President Hunter progressed in his self-discipline and his dedication to the work, he was encouraged and motivated by the examples set by his apostolic brethren, especially by those who had later become the President of the Church. President Hunter described an experience near Christmastime in 1968 when the Apostles gathered in the apartment of President David O. McKay in the Hotel Utah to wish him a merry Christmas. As they surrounded the prophet, each spoke a few words of gratitude for President McKay and bore testimony about the Savior. "This deeply touched the President," wrote Elder Hunter, "and he wept as he made the statement that in all the world there is no other group like this, brethren who love each other and love the Lord. With tears streaming down his face, he prayed that the Lord would make him worthy of the confidence of the brethren. It was a moving occasion, and the Spirit bore witness to me that we were sitting in the presence of the Lord's Prophet upon the earth."

President Hunter had another epiphany at the time of the death of President Joseph Fielding Smith, who died quietly and suddenly just two weeks shy of this ninety-sixth birthday while living in the home of his daughter Amelia McConkie and her husband, Elder Bruce R. McConkie of the Twelve. His daughter had been in the living room with her father and stepped out momentarily. When she returned he was slumped over and was gone. On being advised of the circumstances of his passing, Elder Hunter wrote: "I have often wondered about the condition of persons who are translated and tonight I have had the feeling that this was the course the President has followed from mortality to immortality without tasting of death."

During the years of his apostolic service, Elder Hunter served longer under the prophetic direction of Spencer W. Kimball than any other President of the Church. It also appears he had a more intimate relationship with him than any other prophet, given the lengthy tour of the Holy Land they took together with their wives and their association in the events and procedures leading up to the creation of the Orson Hyde Monument and the BYU Jerusalem Center on the Mount of Olives. Moreover, Elder Hunter was involved with President Kimball in the significant events surrounding the receipt of the revelation on priesthood announced in June 1978.

There had been discussions among the brethren for many years about this matter. These became poignant in the early 1960s, when numerous letters were received at Church headquarters from Nigeria and Ghana urgently requesting the Church to send missionaries. It was painful for the brethren to decline these requests. They did so because the restrictions on blacks holding the priesthood would prevent the full establishment of the Church there. Later, when a mission president in Brazil asked about giving the priesthood to blacks, President David O. McKay wrote: "Preach the gospel to them, but for the present, until the Lord gives us another revelation, those who have negro blood are not to receive the priesthood" (David O. McKay diary, October 4, 1960, quoted in Gibbons, *David O. McKay: Apostle to the World, Prophet of God*, 384).

This issue was wrenching to President Kimball, who had received a special commission to nurture minorities throughout the world from President George Albert Smith. His apostolic assignment to oversee the work in South America had given him special empathy for those barred from the priesthood because of the Church's policy. This was especially true in Brazil where so many were affected by the policy and where, in 1966, President Kimball had created the São Paulo Stake, the first stake in South America.

In the late 1970s, President Kimball's concern about the policy escalated as work on the temple in São Paulo progressed. That concern focused on the difficulty to be faced by the local leaders in determining who could and who could not receive the priesthood blessings of the temple. It was exacerbated by the prophet's call to all the Church to join him in praying that the doors of all nations would be opened to the preaching of the gospel, knowing full well this would be ineffectual in Africa as long as the Church's policy on blacks and the priesthood remained unchanged. These factors drove President Kimball to his knees, imploring the Lord for the revelation to which President McKay had alluded. These included lengthy, fervent prayers in the holy temple. Very soon he involved his counselors in the process and later Elder Hunter and the other members of the Twelve. On April 20, 1978, the prophet advised the Twelve of his prayerful efforts to receive divine guidance on the issue and asked them to join him and his counselors in their efforts toward that end. Elder Hunter recounted a private interview he had with the prophet on this subject, noting, "I could feel his deep concern and his desire to follow strictly the will of the Lord."

Two weeks after President Kimball invited the Twelve to join him and his counselors in their prayers concerning priesthood restrictions, an incident of signal importance occurred. On May 4, 1978, following a council meeting, Elder LeGrand Richards asked President Kimball for the privilege of saying a few words. He told the Brethren that during the meeting, he saw a personage seated in a chair by the organ. He said he thought it was President Wilford

Woodruff. "He was dressed in a white suit and was seated in an armchair" reported Elder Richards. "I thought at the time that the reason I was privileged to see him was probably that I was the only one there who had ever seen President Woodruff while he was upon the earth. I had heard him dedicate the Salt Lake Temple and I had heard him give his last sermon in the Salt Lake Tabernacle before he died" (Tate, *LeGrand Richards: Beloved Apostle*, 292). The significance and timing of this appearance are apparent. Here, appearing through the veil in the upper room of the temple, was the prophet who almost a hundred years before had wrestled with a critical problem, plural marriage, which was resolved by revelation, the same way the problem President Kimball faced would be resolved.

The week following this incident, President Kimball again spent several hours alone in the temple asking the Lord for guidance. On Tuesday May 30, 1978, he read to his counselors a tentative statement he had written in longhand, removing all priesthood restrictions from blacks, except those restrictions regarding worthiness which rest upon all alike. He said that he had "a good warm feeling" about it. The luncheon in the temple for the following Thursday, June 1, was canceled. The Apostles were asked to come to the meeting fasting. At this meeting each member of the council expressed himself freely on the subject. Following the prayer offered by President Kimball, a powerful confirming spirit was felt by all. Of the occasion Elder Hunter wrote: "Following the prayer there were many expressions of love and appreciation among the brethren. Comments were made about the feeling shared by all, that seldom, if ever, had there been greater unanimity in the council."

On Wednesday, June 7, 1978, President Kimball advised his counselors that through inspiration he was moved to lift the restrictions on priesthood. At the time, letters were read from three members of the Twelve, which President Kimball had requested, containing suggested wording for the public announcement of the revelation on priesthood. Using these three letters as a base, a fourth statement was prepared and then reviewed, edited, and approved by the First Presidency. This document was taken to the council meeting with the Twelve on Thursday, June 8, 1978. At this meeting President Kimball advised the Twelve that he had received the inspiration to make the priesthood available to all worthy male members of the Church, whereupon the document was read and with minor editorial changes was approved. Later in the day Elder Mark E. Petersen approved by telephone from South America, and later Elder Delbert L. Stapley approved when President Spencer W. Kimball visited him in the hospital. The statement, of course, was merely a memorandum of the revelation President Kimball had received by the spiritual means already described.

The next day, Friday, June 9, 1978, all the General Authorities who were in the city and available assembled at 7:00 A.M. President Kimball announced the revelation to lift priesthood restrictions, had the statement read, and invited the comments of the Brethren. All sustained the revelation and approved the statement. The members of the Seventy who were out of the city on assignment were advised of the revelation by telephone. Following the meeting, the statement announcing the revelation was released to the press.

Elder Hunter and his brethren of the Twelve were pleased with the response to the announcement of the revelation. With two exceptions, the thousands of messages received at Church headquarters following the press release were positive. They also were grateful for the way in which the Lord had inspired the prophet and had borne witness to them that the revelation was from Him.

CHAPTER TWELVE

The Razor's Edge

Some people have the misconception that the Apostles are immune from the trials and tribulations of life. They are seen usually in their official capacity on the stand, in the pulpit or mingling with the members before and after meetings. In these settings they are well-dressed, affable, and often smiling, never revealing any sadness or pressure they may be enduring. Seldom does the public learn of the downside of an Apostle's life or that of his family. Often such insight is not obtained until after death, revealing qualities of character which add special luster to lives well-lived amid sunshine and shadow. Such is the case with Howard W. Hunter.

Howard and Claire were free from serious physical ailments until the early 1970s. At that time Claire began to experience temporary episodes of memory loss, accompanied by severe headaches and mild disorientation. By October 1972, her condition was serious enough to require a battery of tests in the hospital. Howard reported that the doctor "diagnosed her condition as hardening of the arteries and prescribed medicine to help overcome the problem." This commenced an eleven-year medical odyssey during which Claire experienced a roller-coaster ride of physical pain and emotional swings which lasted until her death in 1983. During all this time Howard stood helpless to impede the progress of her ailment, other than to exercise his faith in her behalf, provide her with numerous priesthood blessings, and to give heroic support through his prayers and frequent visitations. And, during the latter part of Claire's illness, Howard began his own medical odyssey.

Claire underwent her first surgery on New Years' Day 1976. On that day the surgeon implanted a shunt in her head to relieve the pressure. Howard had agonized about authorizing this procedure. However, during the surgery a quiet feeling of peace came to him, signifying that the procedure was appropriate. Claire was hospitalized for two weeks following the surgery. Each morning, noon, and night Howard visited Claire, remaining with her at night until the closing hour. For ten weeks following her return home, Howard cared for her personal needs. At the end of this period, he took Claire to the doctor for a checkup. The results were disappointing. "He said there should have been greater signs of improvement by this time, which may indicate that the accomplishment will be minimal."

During Claire's hospital stay it was discovered she had diabetes. For a while Howard was able to manage her care, but it soon became apparent he needed help in the home. At first a caregiver came to stay during the day. Ultimately it became necessary to fix an apartment in the basement to provide accommodations for around-the-clock assistance, although Howard provided the care at night.

Meanwhile, Howard continued to fill his apostolic responsibilities. Occasionally a grandchild would accompany him on his assignments. While away from Salt Lake City he called home frequently to check on Claire's condition. She continued to worsen, having a series of small strokes which, in turn, brought on fainting spells. Then further surgery became necessary when one of her lungs collapsed. In May 1981, Claire suffered a cerebral hemorrhage which sent her back to the hospital. When she was released two weeks later, she left in a wheelchair. She never walked again. Despite the complications of Claire's immobility and her inability to speak, Howard tried to maintain a semblance of routine in the home. Although she could not speak, he talked to Claire, telling of events in the family, or his work at the office, or his apostolic assignments outside the city. He took her to the hairdresser for permanents and shampoos. Once, a neighbor, Dorothy Nielsen, witnessed a touching scene through the Hunters' front window when Howard gently lifted Claire out of her wheelchair and, holding her frail body close, danced momentarily in their living room.

The final change in the arrangements for Claire's care occurred in April 1982 when she suffered another cerebral hemorrhage. Upon her release from the hospital, she was placed in a care facility where constant nursing and medical services were available for her comfort and security. For the next eighteen months Howard followed a loving routine that never varied. At least once or twice each day during that period when he was in the city, he visited Claire. Kissing her tenderly and sitting quietly by her bedside, he would talk to her, relating his daily activities or reporting on the doings of family members and friends. He never received or expected a response to his recitals other than a slight squeeze of the hand or a loving glance. Claire's excitement and pleasure at these daily visits were shown in her quickened alertness and the fondness with which she looked upon her husband, showing a responsiveness reserved only for him.

On Saturday and Sunday, October 8–9, 1983, Elder Hunter presided at the division of the Caldwell Idaho Stake. Immediately following the last session on Sunday, he called Salt Lake to inquire about Claire. Told that she was all right, he caught a flight home and was met at the Salt Lake airport by J. Paulson Hunter, the family doctor. From the doctor's appearance, Howard knew something was amiss. This impression was confirmed with the doctor's first words: "Claire has left us," he said. "She passed away just an hour ago." Elder Hunter was "heartsick" at the news. "I knew that she could not get well, but it did not take away the pain I felt knowing that she was gone." After going to the nursing home to make arrangements for the care of his beloved wife's body, he returned home. It was then the full impact of her passing struck him. "When I got home, the house seemed cold, and as I walked about, everything reminded me of her." Then, following the beautiful funeral services, he wrote with a sense of sad finality, "I was commencing to realize that she will not be back."

At the time of Claire's passing in 1983, Elder Hunter's health was reasonably good. It had been three years since the heart episode of July and August 1980. After six weeks of hospitalization and recuperation at home, he was relieved of boredom and anxiety by returning to work the first week in September. Before this heart attack, Elder Hunter had experienced only two other incidents of serious illness in his entire life. The first was an attack of mumps suffered in February 1977. He was infected while on an assignment in

Mexico. Because mumps usually afflicts only the young, Howard endured some good-natured ribbing from his brethren. Others didn't have the temerity to mention it, at least in his presence. Probably they joined his brethren in chuckling about it. But to him it was no laughing matter because it was painful and held the potential of serious long-term consequences.

The other serious ailment Howard had before the 1980 heart attack was a complicated four-and-a-half-hour surgery on June 7, 1980, to remove a lymph node. Fortunately this proved to be non-cancerous, although that did not diminish the seriousness of the operation, the uncertainty which preceded it, or the discomfort which followed it.

The 1980 heart attack served as a wake-up call for Elder Hunter. Being seventy-three years old at the time, he became aware of the need to guard and to build his health. He began a regimen which he followed faithfully for six years: regular physical exercise, a healthy diet, adequate rest, and regular physical checkups. As a result, Howard looked and felt better than he had in years. Consequently, he was shocked to be told following a routine checkup in October 1986 that he had blocked coronary arteries and that immediate surgery was recommended. Yielding to that recommendation, he underwent a five-hour surgery on October 12, 1986, which entailed a quadruple coronary bypass.

The strength and stamina Howard had built up during the previous six years served him well. He was walking around the hospital within two days after surgery, and after ten days he was walking a mile in the halls. At home he made arrangements to work out at a cardiac rehabilitation center, which built his strength and gave him energy. His secretary, Dorene Beagles, who had replaced Ruth Webb, his secretary for many years, regularly brought him papers from the office for his attention or signature. Security men who were on twenty-four-hour duty at his home provided necessary assistance. Following this regimen, Howard made a quick and apparently complete recovery from the heart surgery so that he looked forward to resuming his duties in 1987. "I am grateful that I will be able to go forward into the new year without any limitation. . . . There is every reason to believe that 1987 will be a good year."

While Howard began the new year with optimism and vigor, the hope of a good year ultimately proved to be ephemeral. On January 22, he and Richard departed for Europe where President Hunter had a series of assignments to fill. From there they traveled to Israel for meetings connected with the Jerusalem Center. The excitement of being back at work on matters of importance was enhanced by Richard's presence, then a successful attorney practicing in California. Father and son cherished the time together, conversing about family, Church, and professional matters.

After his return from the trip with Richard, President Hunter underwent a treadmill test. He was elated to hear the doctor say his heart was in good condition. The euphoria was short-lived. Soon after, he began to suffer severe lower back pains. Tests revealed deterioration in a disc. The doctors decided to forgo surgery for the moment and to monitor Howard's condition. Meanwhile they gave clearance for him to travel to Burma. On April 6, following general conference, these plans were canceled because of severe stomach pains. Tests revealed he had a bleeding ulcer. His condition was thought to be serious enough to require hospitalization. When two days of treatment failed to stanch the bleeding, surgery became necessary. A team of three surgeons performed the three-hour operation. Afterward, heavy medication kept Howard in a mental fog for several days, during which time his surgeons carefully monitored his condition. By April 18 he was back to normal, noting in his journal that he had gone to the hospital for what he was told would be an hour's stay and twelve days later was released, minus part of his stomach. But he was grateful for the skill and dedication of the surgeons and other hospital personnel who undoubtedly had helped prolong his life.

Meanwhile, the condition of his back continued to worsen. On May 11 he was readmitted to the hospital, where he underwent two weeks of therapy designed to help prepare him for the surgery. After two weeks he was released to return home. The plan was for him to remain there for a period of recuperation, gaining sufficient strength to undergo back surgery, following the major abdominal surgery for the ulcer. At home he had around-the-clock nursing care. However, the back pains were so intense that the surgeons decided on an operation after Howard had spent only a week at home. On June 4, 1987, he returned to the hospital for the surgery on his back. Following the surgery, he remained in the intensive care unit for a week and then was placed in a private room where he remained until his release.

The operation was a surgical success. However, its aftermath, accompanied by the onset of diabetes, resulted in constant, intense leg pains. Despite this he soon began working with a therapist who came to his home twice a week to assist in the lengthy rehabilitation which followed. Howard described the process: "I exercise every day. I have arm exercises holding a bean bag, leg exercises pedaling a device like a bicycle, walking on the walker, and other routines to help strengthen my arms and legs." Notwithstanding his heroic efforts, it soon became apparent he would be relegated to a wheelchair.

President Hunter was able to rejoin his brethren in mid-August for their weekly meetings. With only a short while remaining before the October general conference, he began preparations to speak to the Saints for the first time in several months. Meanwhile, members of his quorum arranged for a specially fitted chair which would enable him to speak to the audience while seated. It was with feelings of humility, and not a little trepidation, that President Hunter prepared an address for the conference which, because of the dramatic circumstances under which it was delivered and its profound content, stands as one of the most significant pronouncements made by him from the Tabernacle pulpit during his apostolic ministry. The sermon was titled simply "The Opening and Closing of Doors." After making brief and apologetic remarks about addressing the conference while seated, he moved immediately into the substance of his remarks: "I have observed that life," he began, "every life—has a full share of ups and downs." This signaled his remarks would not dwell upon his own physical misfortunes but rather would focus upon life's challenges from which no one is immune. Continuing, he said, "Indeed, we see many joys and sorrows in the world, many changed plans and new directions, many blessings that do not always look or feel like blessings, and much that humbles us and improves our patience and our faith. We have all had those experiences from time to time, and I suppose we always will" (*Ensign*, November 1987, 54). Having outlined the essence of his message, President Hunter cited the traumatic experiences of other well-known Church leaders: Presidents Spencer W. Kimball, Marion G. Romney, and Elder A. Theodore Tuttle. He quoted the words of Lehi from the Book of Mormon: "'For it must needs be, that there is an opposition in all things. If not so, . . . righteousness could not be brought to pass, neither wickedness, neither holiness nor misery, neither good nor bad' (2 Nephi 2:15)" (Ibid.). After citing the experience of the Prophet Joseph Smith, confined in the squalid Liberty Jail, he said, "Where one door shuts, another opens, even for a prophet in prison" (Ibid.). Finally, he quoted the words of Elder Orson F. Whitney: "'No pain that we suffer, no trial that we experience is wasted. It ministers to our education, to the development of such qualities as patience, faith, fortitude, and humility. All that we suffer and all that we endure, especially when we endure it patiently, builds up our characters, purifies our hearts, expands our souls, and makes us more tender and charitable, more worthy to be called the children of God'" (Ibid.).

In conclusion, President Hunter emphasized that these principles apply to all alike, whatever one's status or station in life: "If you have troubles at home," he said, "with children who stray, if you suffer financial reverses and emotional strain that threaten your homes and your happiness, if you must face the loss of life or health, may peace be unto your soul. We will not be tempted beyond our ability to withstand. Our detours and disappointments are the straight and narrow path to Him" (Ibid.).

The year 1987 in the life of President Hunter is an enigma. It began with his optimism for a good and healthful year but ended in disaster in his health, with two major surgeries which left him in a wheelchair. By his own definition, however, it must be counted as a year of significant value and advantage.

The seeming contradiction of reaping benefit from misfortune is not an unsolvable puzzle but is an illustration of an eternal principle illustrated by President Hunter in his sermon "The Opening and Closing of Doors." Sometimes, he said, traumatic events in life don't look much like blessings. The pain, anguish, and loss of mobility he suffered were devastating. How could these detriments ever be compensated for? Were President Hunter merely a physical being, the answer would be "never." But as an eternal being presently in mortal form and mortal probation, the answer would be to enumerate the spiritual qualities his months of suffering had yielded, the qualities of patience, humility, gentleness, and kindness.

There can be little doubt that President Hunter was a different person after the watershed year of 1987. There seemed to be in him then a sense of calm resignation that had not existed before. In his earlier days he had been resolutely independent, relying chiefly upon himself and the blessings of the Lord to achieve his purposes. At this time there came to him a sense of resignation, a recognition of his physical limitations and a willingness to submit himself to the ministrations of his family and his brethren. It was an endearing quality which would remain with him throughout the rest of his life. He had gone through the refining fire of adversity and had emerged purged of physical dross. The remainder of his life would consist of a succession of pleasant days, filled with love and submission to the will of his Lord and Creator. Clouds would encumber some of these days but would never obscure the calm serenity with which he faced the future as one of the Almighty's favored sons.

CHAPTER THIRTEEN

PRESIDENT OF THE TWELVE

For several years Howard served as the Acting President of the Twelve during a period when President Marion G. Romney was physically unable to fulfill that duty. During this time, President Hunter was always respectful of President Romney's apostolic status and seniority. He treasured President Romney's friendship, as he was the first General Authority to visit President Hunter in his home after being called as stake president. Their mutual professional life as attorneys and their similar struggles to obtain their education had created a distinctive bond between them. Thus the passing of his friend and mentor was a personal as well as a fraternal loss.

Because President Hunter had been administering the affairs of the Twelve for some time, his new role did not alter the nature of his work and his responsibility. It did, however, effect a significant change in his apostolic status. As the President of the Twelve he stood in direct line to become the next president of the Church should he survive President Ezra Taft Benson. This awesome prospect added a new layer of apprehension to President Hunter's already intense and complicated life. It meant that at any moment the ultimate earthly responsibility to direct the affairs of an international church would rest upon him. One can only surmise about the mental and spiritual impact upon him of this possibility. It is the sense of the writer that this possibility weighed heavily in the action President Hunter took on April 10, 1990.

President Hunter's first trip abroad after being set apart as the President of the Twelve was to Israel in May 1989, accompanied by his son Richard. The purpose of the trip was the dedication of the Jerusalem Center recounted in Chapter 10. From Israel the travelers went to nearby Jordan to visit members of a small branch in Amman. While there they were hosted at an elaborate dinner by Oli Ghandour, chairman of the board of Royal Jordanian Airlines and Hotels and the former prime minister of Lebanon. Also present were General Hanaidy Jel-Fayez, aide-de-camp to Jordan's King Hussein, and the general's wife. The fact that President Hunter took the time to visit Jordan illustrates his neutral, democratic attitude toward the Jewish-Muslim conflict in the Middle East. From Jordan, President Hunter flew to Frankfurt, Germany, to attend to Church affairs at the temple there and thence to Rotterdam, the Netherlands, where he conducted a regional conference.

Throughout all his years of apostolic service, President Hunter had retained his association with the Beneficial Life Insurance Company, and in July 1989 he attended a convention of the company held in Cancun, Mexico. During the weeks before the semiannual general conference in 1989, he conducted a series of mission, regional, and area meetings in France, Scotland, and England. Again his son Richard was his traveling companion.

Despite the problems presented by his decreased mobility, President Hunter was determined to fulfill his share of the global responsibilities of the Twelve Apostles. As he contemplated the future in the light of his single status, it is inferred that he appraised the impact on the Church of a single man becoming its president. Whatever the reasons which motivated him, it was about this time that President Hunter began to consider the possibility of remarriage. Claire had been gone for nearly seven years. No one could ever take her place as the love of his youth and the mother of his children, nor could their eternal union, formed when they knelt at the altar in the Salt Lake Temple, ever be broken. When President Hunter made the decision to remarry, his attention focused on Inis Stanton, whom he had known many years before in California. Inis was an attractive, outgoing mother of three children who worked as a receptionist in the lobby of the Church Office Building. By early spring 1990, their relationship had progressed to the point that Howard proposed matrimony. Inis, a faithful Latter-day Saint, was honored and pleased to accept.

Both Inis's and Howard's families and President Hunter's brethren were unaware of their budding relationship. Richard was the first member of the Hunter family to learn about it. He had traveled from California to Utah to attend the April 1990 general conference. In a conversation with him, Howard sought Richard's reaction to the possibility of his remarriage. The son responded positively and with encouragement. When Richard asked if he had someone in mind, Howard told him about Inis. Later, at a dinner at which he met Inis, Richard asked if a date for the wedding had been set. "Yes, next Thursday," Howard answered. We are left to surmise about Richard's reaction to this news. Knowing his father as he did, he probably was not surprised.

President Hunter's marriage to Inis Stanton was a great blessing to him, to her, and to the Church. It provided companionship for both of them and, for the entire Church, it set an example of marital joy and compatibility.

It was a pleasant and educational experience for Inis to become adjusted to the nomadic life of a General Authority. Two weeks after their marriage, she accompanied him to a regional conference in Norfolk, Virginia. Setting a pattern for the rest of their life together, she was called upon to speak. This maiden effort at speaking before large audiences was noteworthy. She chose as her subject the phrase "Bloom where you are planted." The essence of her message was that regardless of status or locale, one should work and strive in the place of the moment. It was a testimonial of her own experience. She had come to Salt Lake City alone and unknown. Finding employment, she made her own way, created a circle of new friends and, while active in the Church, took up the hobby of creating beautiful dolls. Their dainty and lifelike appearance and the lively colors and styling of their clothes was of professional quality. Inis later delighted the wives of the General Authorities by exhibiting her dolls and describing the process of creation. Such was the volume of dolls she had made that special renovations were necessary in the Hunter home in order to accommodate and display them.

Inis soon found that her husband was never off duty. The lengthy tour they took five weeks after their marriage was planned as a honeymoon. It was a wonderful trip to exotic places but of necessity was interspersed with apostolic errands. They took a leisurely trip up the Nile from Luxor to Aswan with a BYU tour group. Long, pleasant days on the river afforded many opportunities for conversation and reflection as they passed ancient sites of Egyptian culture and architecture at Luxor, the Valley of the Kings, and the Valley of the Queens. Even there, however, in such a remote place, away from telephones and mail deliveries, President Hunter could not escape the duties of his apostolic calling as the students on the tour were anxious to access his wealth of knowledge and spirituality. They were inspired to hear him pray and to discourse on gospel themes as well as upon archeological matters, to which his long experience with the BYU archeological group had given him special insight.

From Aswan, the Hunters flew to Israel. Here President Hunter had scheduled appointments with those involved with the Church projects on the Mount of Olives. With the assistance of a Latter-day Saint guide, the Hunters visited ancient biblical sites at Galilee, the Jordan River, Jericho, and the Dead Sea, among others. From Israel the travelers flew to England where they visited places of historic interest before returning home.

In November, President and Sister Hunter traveled into the Pacific for a series of regional and stake conferences in Fiji, New Zealand, and Australia. On November 14, they were feted at a birthday dinner at the Sydney Opera House, celebrating President Hunter's eighty-third birthday.

It was satisfying to him that he was able to travel such long distances and to move through airports using only a walker. He had given up his wheelchair at the end of 1988 and continued to work with a therapist in the hope he would be able to walk again. He was encouraged that "with a little help" he was able to stand for the prayer circle of General Authorities in October 1987. His hope of walking unassisted was never realized, but through determined effort he avoided being permanently confined to a wheelchair.

January 1991 brought a nostalgic reward to President Hunter. He and Inis were invited to Los Angeles to participate in the fiftieth anniversary of the South Pasadena Ward, the successor of the El Sereno Ward, whose first bishop was young Howard W. Hunter. Fourteen bishops had served the ward during its fifty-year history, eleven of whom were present for the celebration. President Hunter was the main speaker on this historic occasion. It was a joyous experience to reflect upon the beginnings of this ward and the many choice incidents which had occurred during the interim. Many of the original ward members had returned for the celebration.

The following month brought another celebration for President Hunter when he and Elder M. Russell Ballard and their wives traveled to Merida, Mexico, for a regional conference. Only fourteen years before, President Hunter had organized the Merida Mexico Stake. At the time of this conference, there were four stakes in the region and more than a thousand priesthood leaders gathered at a priesthood leadership meeting on Saturday night of the conference. It was a great source of satisfaction for the two Apostles to observe the phenomenal growth of the Church in this area and similar growth being experienced in different parts of Latin America. During this trip the travelers spent some time in Cancun, Mexico, and visited some of the Mayan archeological sites at Chichén Itzá, which President Hunter had visited many times before.

Three months later, the Hunters embarked on a lengthy trip into South America. Stake or regional conferences were held in São Paulo, Brazil; Buenos Aires, Argentina; and Santiago, Chile. Beautiful temples graced all three of these major South American cities. As a historian, President Hunter doubtless was intrigued by the fact that his friend, President Spencer W. Kimball, had created the first stake and had dedicated the temple in São Paulo, both firsts in all of South America. The site in Buenos Aires where, in 1925, Elder Melvin J. Ballard had dedicated all of South America for the preaching of the gospel was a testimonial of the vigorous growth of the Church and the prophetic insight of Elder M. Russell Ballard's grandfather.

The following month found the Hunters in Alaska for a conference. This great shift in geography in just a month's time must have been a wake-up call for Inis, demonstrating the global scope of her husband's responsibilities. While in Alaska, the Hunters took a cruise of Prince William Sound. Having developed from his youth his powers of observation, combined with his penchant for carefully recording what he saw, these descriptions of what the Hunters saw on their cruise are certainly typical for Howard, "26 glaciers, fjords, waterfalls and wildlife, sea lions, porpoises, seals, sea otters, countless types of birds and mammals, and many species of the wildlife of Alaska. . . . We stopped near cliffs where thousands of kittiwakes and other sea birds were flocking."

President Hunter's independent nature was on full display two weeks after returning from Alaska. As he stood to speak at a dinner honoring Mayor Teddy Kollek who was visiting from Jerusalem, he choked. Rushed to the hospital, it was discovered that a particle of food had aspirated into his lungs. After three days he called the family doctor to say he intended to leave the hospital. The doctor said he would come to discuss the matter with him. President Hunter then called Inis to request that she come to the hospital to drive him home. She and the doctor arrived at about the same time. "I told them I was going home and going to Hawaii tomorrow," President Hunter said. All the medical reasons the doctor could advance failed to persuade him: "When he found I was serious he made arrangements for my release."

The magnet which drew him to Hawaii at this time was a long-planned trip to the islands with his sons and their wives. The following morning he and Inis flew to Los Angeles, where they were joined by Richard and Nan for the flight to Honolulu; John and Louine had traveled earlier. The three couples were feted at a banquet and celebration at the Polynesian Cultural Center. After visiting sites of historic interest on Oahu with the children, President Hunter and Inis flew to Kauai for the annual convention of the Beneficial Life Insurance Company.

The following August while attending a regional conference in Panama City, President Hunter performed one of the most significant acts of his apostolic ministry. With a small group of Saints, he went to the summit of Ancon Hill. There he dedicated the land of the Republic of Panama "to the Lord and for the preaching of the gospel." President Hunter and others of his apostolic brethren, from the time of the organization of the Quorum of the Twelve Apostles in 1835, have ranged over the earth dedicating specific portions of it for this purpose. While in Central America at this time, President Hunter also conducted a regional conference in Guatemala.

President Hunter's last assignment for the year 1991 was to conduct regional conferences in Japan, Hong Kong, and South Korea. It must be remembered that as the President of the Twelve, it was he who made the assignments to members of the Twelve to attend regional and stake conferences in various parts of the world. It is apparent that, despite the physical restrictions imposed upon him by his back problems, he insisted on carrying his full share of assignments.

President Hunter and Inis enjoyed a brief respite from their heavy travel schedule during the month of December. This enabled them to enjoy the peace and quiet of their lovely home for a season.

Their enjoyment was enhanced by a high-tech sound system which carried music and the spoken word throughout the house.

The Hunters' travels during 1992 began with a trip to South Africa for a regional conference in Johannesburg. Accompanied by Elder Boyd K. Packer and his wife, Donna, they went several days early to enable them to visit the famous Kruger National Park. True to form, President Hunter recorded seeing an astonishing variety of animals in the Kruger preserve. One of their most exciting encounters was with a resourceful baboon. The party had been cautioned to keep the windows of their vehicles closed at all times. However, a window was left open as the vehicles were parked on a bridge. President Hunter reported what happened: "A baboon quick as lightning jumped through the window, lifted the lid from the ice chest and grabbed some bags of fruit and the chips. He sat on the bridge, peeled the banana and ate the fruit and the chips. We made a getaway and didn't open the windows again."

Following the conference, the Hunters flew to Frankfurt where they met Elder James E. Faust and his wife, Ruth. The four then flew to Israel. By prearrangement, the Apostles met with Chaim Herzog, president of the state of Israel, giving him a four-volume set of *The Encyclopedia of Mormonism*. The gift had been carefully selected as Mr. Herzog had been the chief editor of the *Encyclopedia Judaica*. This courtesy call enabled the Brethren to make a personal report about the progress of the Jerusalem Center and to express gratitude for the beneficial assistance of the Israeli government in various phases of its construction and development.

Later, the Apostles hosted a luncheon at the Jerusalem Center attended by Mayor Teddy Kollek and officials of the Jerusalem Symphony Association. There a verbal invitation was extended to the Tabernacle Choir to perform in Israel. When the Apostles departed Israel they took with them an official invitation addressed to the First Presidency. That invitation was accepted and on December 26, the Tabernacle Choir performed its first program in the Holy Land.

In May 1992, President Hunter was pleased to join Inis in attending a reunion of the Garvanza Ward in Los Angeles, which she had attended in her youth. Because the El Sereno Ward, where he had served as the first bishop, was nearby, President Hunter knew most of those in attendance. It was a pleasant event for both of them, as Inis enjoyed pointing out places and recalling events which had been of importance during her youth.

The Hunters flew to Wales in May 1992 for a regional conference at Merthyr Tydfil. Here at the birthplace of Jennette Evans McKay, President David O. McKay's mother, stood a charming little chapel which President McKay had dedicated thirty years before. A plaque posted at a humble dwelling in town marked the birthplace of the prophet's mother, born on August 23, 1850. While no record remains of the sermons delivered at this regional conference, it is a safe assumption that President Hunter might have made reference to his mentor, President McKay, and to President McKay's mother, Jennette Evans, whose family was converted by two unknown missionaries laboring in Wales over a hundred years previous.

Accompanying President Hunter for this regional conference was Elder Jeffrey R. Holland of the Seventy, who presided over the area. Following the conference, the two General Authorities drove from Wales into Scotland where they visited Hunterston Castle, the family manor of some of President Hunter's ancestors. A special relationship existed between President Hunter and Elder Holland, arising out of Elder Holland's service as the president of Brigham Young University and his involvement in the creation of the Orson

Hyde Monument and the Jerusalem Center on the Mount of Olives. During his short tenure as the President of the Church, President Hunter called only one man as a member of the Twelve. That man was Jeffrey R. Holland.

From June to September 1992, there was a hiatus in the international travels of President and Sister Hunter, occasioned by Inis undergoing knee surgery. Apart from the pain and discomfort she suffered in the aftermath of the surgery, the situation created problems for Howard as well. Because he could not drive and with Inis incapacitated, moving about created problems. This was alleviated by assistance from family members, thoughtful neighbors, and Church security personnel who assisted occasionally. President Hunter's faithful secretary, Dorene Beagles, also eased his administrative workload in many ways.

The Hunters were on the road again in early September 1992, Inis having had completely recovered. Their destination was eastern Europe for a series of meetings and events in Russia, Ukraine, Armenia, and Austria. President Hunter was surprised to find an audience of 500 at a gathering in Moscow. He was even more surprised to find an audience of 1,200 at the October Palace in Kiev, the capital of Ukraine, where he and Elder Robert K. Dellenbach of the European Area Presidency were the speakers. A highlight of this trip occurred on September 12, 1992, when President Hunter dedicated Austria for the preaching of the gospel. The site for the ceremony was the top of a hill in the Vienna woods, overlooking the city of Vienna and the beautiful Danube River. Their tour ended with a regional conference in Munich where 4,000 were gathered in a sports arena for the general session.

The Hunters ended their travels for 1992 with a trip to London for a regional conference and the rededication of the London

Temple and then a trip to the Pacific for a series of meetings. A few days after Thanksgiving, in Salt Lake City, President Hunter entered the hospital because of internal bleeding. He remained for two weeks.

On February 7, 1993, President Hunter had the unsettling experience previously mentioned when a man accosted him during a speech at the Marriott Center at Brigham Young University, threatening to detonate a bomb unless President Hunter read a letter thrust before him. He calmly and quietly refused. During the ten-minute interval before the assailant was subdued, there was pandemonium in the auditorium. Some panicked and fled in tears. Others brought a semblance of order by singing the hymns "We Thank Thee, O God, for a Prophet" and "I Am a Child of God." There was scuffling on the stand as efforts were made to restrain the assailant. He finally was subdued and removed after a student sprayed him with mace. Throughout all this President Hunter retained an icy calm while remaining standing at the pulpit. When it was all over, he continued his speech as previously described.

It must be assumed that President Hunter was frightened by the incident. How could he not have been? Yet he retained his poise and composure in the same manner as his predecessor and hero Joseph Smith had done when he rode to his death in Carthage, "as calm as a summer's morning." Although President Hunter did not forfeit his life at this time, it is plain he was prepared to do so, refusing to read the words of a demented man, even under threat of death.

In May 1993, President Hunter underwent what was thought to be routine gall bladder surgery. The surgery was successful, but Howard failed to revive from the anesthesia afterward. For twenty days he seemed poised on the brink of death. Indeed, one doctor opined that he would never recover. But it was not his time to go. He still had important work to do. At the end of twenty days, he awakened with full mentality and was interested to be briefed about what had occurred during his long sleep.

Through the years of his apostolic ministry, President Hunter received several recognitions for his service, including honorary doctoral decrees from Brigham Young University and BYU–Hawaii. He also was honored to receive the Exemplary Manhood Award from the Brigham Young University Student Association for the academic year 1992–1993. Three recognitions he received during his service as the President of the Twelve were of special significance to him. First was the Howard W. Hunter professorship created at the J. Reuben Clark Law School at BYU. He was pleased when he later learned that the Watson Land Company contributed $50,000 toward funding the professorship in recognition of his long service to that company. He was pleased also by the brochure his son Richard prepared for the occasion which outlined significant events in his father's life. Second, a similar professorship was created in the Mormon Studies department at Claremont Graduate University in California. Third, on November 26, 1990, the Ninth Circuit Court of Appeals in Los Angeles issued a citation recognizing President Hunter's fifty years of "dedication and service to the administration of justice" as a member of the bar of the court.

CHAPTER FOURTEEN

PRESIDENT OF THE CHURCH

The moment President Hunter had not sought for but which had been decreed for him by destiny occurred on May 30, 1994, the day of the death of President Ezra Taft Benson. At the moment of President Benson's death, Howard W. Hunter became the de facto president of the Church. Although President Hunter had been aware this was a real possibility, when it happened he was shocked and full of emotion. We are left to conjecture as to the thoughts which filled his mind at the time. The enormity of the responsibility which was now his surely was at the forefront. He was now the ultimate earthly authority for the governance of a worldwide and rapidly growing church. He was answerable only to the divine head of the Church, the Lord Jesus Christ. Having exercised apostolic authority for thirty-six years and having observed firsthand the methods of five preceding prophets—David O. McKay, Joseph

Fielding Smith, Harold B. Lee, Spencer W. Kimball, and Ezra Taft Benson—President Hunter knew instinctively the course he would follow. That course would be to emulate the character of his Savior Jesus Christ and to live in such a way as to be able to receive the revelation necessary to guide the Church aright.

President Hunter's first duty was to arrange, preside at, and speak at funeral services recognizing the apostolic service of President Benson. At these services, held June 4, 1994, in the Salt Lake Tabernacle, President Hunter paid tribute to his friend and mentor: "My heart is heavy today," he began, "at the passing of our beloved prophet and President, Ezra Taft Benson. We have lost a dear friend, a wise and experienced associate in the presiding councils of the Church and an inspired prophet of God. We miss him deeply on this day in which we have gathered to pay our last respects to him. I feel his loss in a particularly personal way. For nearly thirty-five years we sat together in the Council of the Twelve Apostles. He was always sensitive and kind to me and to all of his brethren in the sweet association we have there. For ten of those years, President Benson presided over the Council of the Twelve. Oh, how we thrilled at his guidance. He was a gifted leader, a superb administrator. We all felt the keenness of his mind and the power of his priesthood as he led us. I saw the mantle of prophetic leadership settle upon his shoulders. I felt his humility and his dependence on the Lord as he stepped into the sacred office he would now hold. I heard his voice rise to new levels of spiritual eloquence and divine utterance. Now that mighty voice is stilled, and we mourn with the entire Church at the silence."

After those eloquent words lauding his mentor's life and service, President Hunter spoke feelingly of the prophet's love for his wife, Flora, who preceded him in death: "Although this is a time of sadness, it thrills us to think of the joyful reunion President Benson is having with his beloved sweetheart, Flora, who has been waiting patiently—or perhaps a little impatiently—for her husband of sixty-six years to join her on the other side. Theirs was a storybook romance, an example to all of what a marriage should be. Until Sister Benson's passing, they were absolutely inseparable. And even when the weight of his office was particularly heavy in those later years, they still went to the temple together every Friday morning. They continued that sweet practice until Sister Benson could no longer physically make the journey." Then, addressing the children and grandchildren, he admonished them to "perpetuate his testimony, his teachings, and the loyalty he gave to your family circle" ("'A Strong and Mighty Man,'" *Ensign*, July 1994, 41–42).

President Hunter reflected upon some of the important subjects and themes President Benson had dwelled upon during the course of his apostolic ministry, upon missionary work, upon the family, and upon the Book of Mormon. As to the latter, he quoted President Benson as saying, "'The Book of Mormon must be reenthroned in the minds and hearts of our people. We must honor it by reading, by studying it, by taking its precepts into our lives and transforming them into lives required of the true followers of Christ.' He never tired of reminding us that the Prophet Joseph Smith himself had said, 'the Book of Mormon was the most correct of any book on earth, and the keystone of our religion, and a man would get nearer to God by abiding by its precepts, than by any other book'" (Ibid.).

President Hunter concluded his eulogy of the deceased prophet by referring to the keys of authority he held: "I testify," he said, "that the prophetic keys which he held were unbroken from the Prophet Joseph Smith down to his own receipt of them, and that those keys and that office will continue, unbroken, to another and another until the Savior himself will come to reign as King of Kings and Lord of Lords. This is Christ's church, and we are his prophets" (Ibid.).

On June 5, 1994, the day following the funeral, the fourteen Apostles gathered in the Upper Room of the Salt Lake Temple for a council meeting. They sat in upholstered chairs arranged in a semicircle facing the three empty chairs near the west wall which are normally occupied by the members of the First Presidency. On the wall behind the three chairs were paintings depicting the Savior and on other walls of the room were portraits of the first thirteen presidents of the restored Church. The first order of business was to consider the reorganization of the First Presidency. This conformed with the long-established practice of promptly reorganizing the First Presidency following the death of the prophet. The worldwide interests and demands of the Church made this a vital necessity. Following discussion it was the unanimous sense that the reorganization not be delayed, whereupon Elder Gordon B. Hinckley, the second apostle in terms of seniority, nominated Howard William Hunter as the President of the Church. There being a second, Howard W. Hunter was unanimously sustained as the fourteenth President of The Church of Jesus Christ of Latter-day Saints. After President Hunter sat in a chair in the center of the room, all the Apostles placed their hands upon his head and, with Elder Hinckley acting as voice, he was ordained and set apart as the President of the Church, the fourteenth in a direct and unbroken line extending from the Prophet Joseph Smith, the Church's first president. By this action the suspended authority to lead the Church which had been conferred upon President Hunter at the time he was inducted into the Quorum of the Twelve was ratified. At this same meeting President Hunter called Gordon B. Hinckley as the First

Counselor and Thomas S. Monson as the Second Counselor in the First Presidency. They were duly confirmed by the Apostles and set apart. President Hinckley was also confirmed and set apart as the President of the Quorum of the Twelve Apostles, and Boyd K. Packer as Acting President of that quorum. Following these important and historic actions, several procedural matters that were necessary for the efficient transfer of authority to the new administration were addressed. All the brethren—indeed the entire Church—were impressed and inspired by this simple yet majestic procedure in the transfer of such vast worldwide authority without any semblance of bickering or discord, accompanied by expressions and demonstrations of love and amity.

Soon after the ceremony in the Upper Room, President Hunter and his counselors held a press conference where the newly anointed prophet made public expression about his feelings at this significant moment in Church history and, through the members of the media present, sent a significant prophetic message to members of the Church around the globe: "I have shed many tears," he began, "and have sought my Father in Heaven in earnest prayer with a desire to be equal to the high and holy calling which is now mine. My greatest strength through these past hours and recent days has been my abiding testimony that this is the work of God and not men, that Jesus Christ is the authorized and living head of this church and He leads it in word and deed. I pledge my life, my strength, and the full measure of my soul to serving Him fully." Having thus borne his personal witness of the reality of Jesus Christ as the living head of the Church, President Hunter then delivered a message to the members of the Church living around the world and to all people. Said he, "To the membership of the Church in every country of the world and to people everywhere I extend my love. . . . I pray that we might treat each other with more kindness, more courtesy, more humility and patience and forgiveness. . . . I invite the members of the Church to establish the temple of the Lord as the great symbol of their membership and the supernal setting for their most sacred covenants. It would be the deepest desire of my heart to have every member of the Church be temple worthy. I would hope that every adult member would be worthy of—and carry—a current temple recommend, even if proximity to a temple does not allow immediate or frequent use of it" (in Jay M. Todd, "President Howard W. Hunter: Fourteenth President of the Church," *Ensign*, July 1994, 2).

Mention has been made already about the astute aspects of President Hunter's leadership and teaching skills. While he focused here only on the temple and the temple recommend, he by implication also referred to the personal qualifications a member must have or measure up to in order to receive a temple recommend. In his admonition to be more kindly disposed toward others, we also perceive the charitable qualities in his own character.

One of President Hunter's first official acts as the prophet was to call Elder Jeffrey R. Holland of the Seventy to fill the vacancy in the Twelve. Elder Holland was ordained an Apostle on June 23, 1994, in the Upper Room of the Salt Lake Temple by President Hunter and inducted into the Quorum of the Twelve Apostles. The sacred apostolic oath administered to and accepted by Elder Holland was a reminder to all the Apostles assembled on this occasion of their duties of collegiality, confidentiality, unity, and dedication.

Three days after Elder Holland's ordination, President Hunter was in Nauvoo, Illinois, for the commemoration of the martyrdom of Joseph and Hyrum Smith. With President Hunter were President Gordon B. Hinckley, First Counselor in the First Presidency, and Elder M. Russell Ballard of the Twelve. Three meetings were held by the prophet and his companions during this visit. The first was a special sacrament meeting on Sunday, June 26, held in the Nauvoo stake center. This service and the two meetings held the following day commemorated the 150th anniversary of the martyrdom of the Prophet Joseph Smith and his brother Hyrum. At the Sunday service the prophet expounded on the four pillars of the Church, the first being that the Prophet Joseph Smith in reality saw the Father and the Son in the Sacred Grove; second, that the Book of Mormon is a true record of ancient civilizations which peopled the American Continent; third, that the Holy Priesthood has been restored through the ministrations of heavenly beings; and fourth, that "the pillar of faith related to salvation for the dead" allowed everyone to receive, through direct or proxy means, the saving ordinances of the gospel ("'The Pillars of Our Faith,'" *Ensign*, September 1994, 54). This fourth pillar was elaborated upon at a meeting held in mid-afternoon the following day when about 2,500 gathered at the site of the Nauvoo Temple. During this service one of the original sunstones which had adorned the Nauvoo temple before its destruction was unveiled. This unveiling reminded the audience of the beautiful temple which had once stood there and of its symbolic and real significance to the members of the Church. Referring to the Prophet Joseph Smith's attitude toward the temple, President Hunter said: "He wanted a temple completed so that there could be elders who, having received the ordinances of the endowment, could then better help establish Zion. Near this very site, Joseph spoke of the need to 'build up stakes in all North and South America.' . . . In fulfillment of his prophetic statement, we now have 1,714 stakes on this hemisphere" ("The Temple of Nauvoo," *Ensign*, September 1994, 62).

Alluding to his earlier statement about temple worthiness,

ent Hunter said: "As you know, earlier this month I began my try by expressing a deep desire to have more and more Church members become temple worthy. As in Joseph's day, having worthy and endowed members is the key to building the kingdom in all the world. Temple worthiness ensures that our lives are in harmony with the will of the Lord, and we are attuned to receive His guidance in our lives" (Ibid.).

President Hunter then paid personal tribute to the Prophet Joseph Smith, whose life had been taken 150 years before by a murderous mob. Referring to the hymn "Praise to the Man" which had been sung by the audience, he said, "We praise him for his capacity to commune not only with Jehovah but also with other personages of heaven. So many visited, gave keys, and tutored that 'choice seer' raised up in the latter days." He also said, "We praise the Prophet Joseph Smith, too, for his diligence, . . . [and not only] his capacity to endure but to 'endure it well.'" Of the impact of Joseph Smith's ministry upon him personally, President Hunter said, "The responsibility I feel for the work the Prophet Joseph inaugurated fills me with a determination to do all I can in the time and season allotted to me. Surely Joseph was faithful and true to his time and season!" ("The Temple of Nauvoo," *Ensign*, September 1994, 63).

At the final meeting of the commemoration of the martyrdom of Joseph and Hyrum held near the Carthage Jail, President Hunter elaborated upon the theme of his prophetic ministry first announced at the press conference following his ordination. He said: "This world needs the gospel of Jesus Christ as restored through the Prophet Joseph Smith. The gospel provides the only way the world will ever know peace. We need to be kinder with one another, more gentle and more forgiving. We need to be slower to anger and more prompt to help. We need to extend the hand of friendship and resist the hand of retribution. In short, we need to love one another with the pure love of Christ, with genuine charity and compassion and, if necessary, shared suffering, for that is the way God loves us" ("Come to the God of All Truth," *Ensign*, September 1994, 72).

President Hunter's first written message to the members of the Church was titled "The Great Symbol of Our Membership." It began, "At the time of my call to this sacred office, an invitation was given for all members of the Church to establish the temple of the Lord as the great symbol of their membership and the supernal setting for their most sacred covenants" (*Ensign*, October 1994, 2–5). He portrayed the temple as a place of instruction, a place of peace, and a place where we make covenants and receive promises conditioned upon our obedience and diligence. As to these conditional promises, he invited the reader to "consider the lifestyle we must live in order to be beneficiaries of these promises." Here the prophet illustrated again his knack of teaching by indirection, the word *lifestyle* alluding indirectly to the conditions which must be met in order to receive a temple recommend. The prophet then expressed the desire of the Lord and his own personal desire that Church members make a commitment to temple worship: "Truly, the Lord desires that His people be a temple-motivated people. It would be the deepest desire of my heart to have every member of the Church be temple worthy. I would hope that every adult member would be worthy of—and carry—a current temple recommend, even if proximity to a temple does not allow immediate or frequent use of it. Let us be a temple-attending and a temple-loving people. Let us hasten to the temple as frequently as time and means and personal circumstances allow. Let us go not only for our kindred dead, but let us also go for the personal blessing of temple worship, for the sanctity and safety which is provided within those hallowed and consecrated walls. The temple is a place of beauty, it is a place of revelation, it is a place of peace. It is the house of the Lord. It is holy unto the Lord. It should be holy unto us" (Ibid.).

At the Solemn Assembly held in the Salt Lake Tabernacle on October 1 and 2, 1994, President Howard W. Hunter was sustained as the fourteenth President of The Church of Jesus Christ of Latter-day Saints, with President Gordon B. Hinckley and President Thomas S. Monson as his counselors. At the same time, Elder Jeffrey R. Holland was sustained as the newest member of the Quorum of the Twelve Apostles.

In his remarks following the sustaining vote of the conference, President Hunter humbly acknowledged his dependence upon the Lord and bore testimony "that this is the work of God and not of men" and that "Jesus Christ is the head of this church" and "leads it in word and deed" ("'Exceeding Great and Precious Promises,'" *Ensign*, November 1994, 7). President Hunter also acknowledged the occasions when he had hovered near death and how his life had been preserved by the blessings of the Lord and the prayers and the faith of the members of the Church.

In his first sermon after being sustained as the President of the Church, President Hunter took up again the subject of the temple, adding new perspectives and insights to what he had previously said about it: "If proximity to a temple does not allow frequent attendance," he said, "gather in the history of your family and prepare the names for the sacred ordinances performed only in the temple. This family research is essential to the work of the temples, and blessings surely will come to those who do that work" (Ibid., 8). After assuring his audience that the Church would continue to accelerate the construction of new temples so as to bring them "closer to our people," the prophet elaborated upon the impact of temple ordinances on the family: "In the ordinances of the temple," he said, "the foundations of the eternal family are sealed in place. The Church has the responsibility—and the authority—to preserve and protect the family as the foundation of society. The pattern for family life, instituted before the foundation of the world, provides for children to be born to and nurtured by a father and mother who are husband and wife, lawfully married. Parenthood is a sacred obligation and privilege, with children welcomed as a 'heritage of the Lord' (Ps. 127:3)" (Ibid.). With prophetic insight, President Hunter alluded to events which threatened the disintegration of the family: "A worried society now begins to see that the disintegration of the family brings upon the world the calamities foretold by the prophets. The world's councils and deliberations will succeed only when they define the family as the Lord has revealed it to be. 'Except the Lord build the house, they labour in vain that build it' (Ps. 127:1)" (Ibid.).

The prophet also focused on the impact of these teachings upon the world. He said: "As we become more removed from the lifestyle of the world, the Church becomes more the welcome refuge for hundreds of thousands who come each year and say, 'Let us go up to the mountain of the Lord, to the house of the God of Jacob: and he will teach us of his ways, and we will walk in his paths: for out of Zion shall go forth the law, and the word of the Lord from Jerusalem' (Isa. 2:3)" (Ibid.).

President Hunter bore his testimony, a testimony which acquires special significance because the prophet would not live to participate in another general conference. He said, "My brothers and sisters, I testify that the impressions of the Spirit have weighed heavily upon me in considering these matters. Our Eternal Heavenly Father lives. Jesus Christ, our Savior and Redeemer, guides his church today through his prophets. Let us, as Latter-day Saints, claim these 'exceeding great and precious promises' so that we, 'Holy Father, . . . may grow up in thee, and receive a fulness of the Holy Ghost, and be organized according to thy laws, and be prepared to obtain every needful thing' (D&C 109:14–15)" (Ibid.).

A week following the general conference, President Hunter dedicated the temple in Orlando, Florida, the forty-sixth operating temple of the Church. During twelve dedicatory sessions held from October 9–11, 1994, more than 20,000 members from the temple district attended the sacred ceremonies. President Hunter was accompanied by his wife, Inis, and by his counselors, Gordon B. Hinckley and Thomas S. Monson, and their wives and other General Authorities and their wives. The prophet spoke and then offered the dedicatory prayer at the first session. Alluding to the picturesque setting of the striking white building, located on a knoll overlooking a chain of placid lakes, the prophet said of the holy edifice, "To all who look upon it, may it ever present a picture of peace and beauty, a structure partaking of Thy divine nature."

A week after dedicating the Orlando Florida Temple, President and Sister Hunter attended the conference of the Pasadena California Stake—the stake where President Hunter presided from 1950–59. When word got out that President Hunter would preside at the conference, former members of the stake flocked from afar to attend. The prophet was received with great love and admiration. During remarks made at the general session of the conference, President Hunter recalled the significant impact upon his life and ministry of the service he had rendered there years before.

In preparing an article for publication in the *Ensign*, President Hunter took up a subject which seems to have dominated his thinking since being ordained as the prophet—the holy temple. He titled the article "A Temple-Motivated People." In it he sketched the theological foundations of vicarious temple ordinances, the holy endowment, and celestial marriage. Of these he wrote, "In the ordinances of the temple, the foundations of the eternal family are sealed in place. The Church has the responsibility—and the authority—to preserve and protect the family as the foundation of society" (*Ensign*, February 1995, 3). In this significant article, President Hunter was moved to repeat what had almost become his mantra since becoming President of the Church. He wrote: "I repeat what I have said before: It would please the Lord for every adult member to be worthy of—and to carry—a current temple recommend, even if proximity to a temple does not allow immediate or frequent use of it. The things that we must do and not do to be worthy of a temple recommend are the very things that ensure we will be happy as individuals and as families" (Ibid., 5).

The prophet flew to Hawaii later in November 1994. There, on November 18, he installed Eric B. Shumway as the eighth president of BYU–Hawaii. He admonished the new leader to "'build faith in . . . the great principles which lead to eternal life which come to us from the prophets of God, both anciently and in our time'" ("News of the Church," *Ensign*, February 1995, 79). It was rejuvenating for the prophet to be back in the setting where he had worked so long in helping to establish the Polynesian Cultural Center on a firm foundation.

A satellite broadcast on November 12, 1994, commemorated the 100th anniversary of the Genealogical Society. It also celebrated President Hunter's eighty-seventh birthday, which occurred on November 14. Participating with the prophet on this occasion were his counselors, Presidents Gordon B. Hinckley and Thomas S. Monson, and Elder Russell M. Nelson of the Twelve, all of whom spoke. In his remarks, President Hunter alluded to the preeminent emphasis given to genealogical and temple work by Joseph Smith, Brigham Young, and all the Presidents of the Church. He also recalled his service as the president of the Genealogical Society and marveled at the acceleration given to the work by the use of modern technological advances. "I look back in wonder," he said, "at the tapestry woven by the Lord in the furthering of temple and family history work" ("We Have a Work to Do," *Ensign*, March 1995, 64). In assessing the enormous task remaining for leaders of the present and the future in pursuing this work, he observed: "We who live in this day are those whom God appointed before birth to be his representatives on earth in this dispensation. We are the house of Israel. In our hands lie the sacred powers of being saviors on Mount Zion in the latter days" (Ibid.).

The prophet said he had "one overriding message" to deliver on this occasion: "This work must hasten. The work waiting to be done is staggering and escapes human comprehension." After referring to the staggering imbalance between the vicarious work performed the previous year and the number of persons who died during that period, he added: "This might suggest futility in the work, . . . but we cannot think of futility. Surely the Lord will support us if we use our best efforts in carrying out the commandment to do family history research and temple work" (Ibid.).

On Sunday, January 8, 1995, President Hunter led a group of General Authorities and their wives to Bountiful, Utah, for the dedication of the forty-seventh operating temple of the Church. Before its dedication, 870,000 people had toured the premises of this beautiful building set high on the eastern foothills of the city. The proceedings of the first dedicatory session were carried by direct video feed to congregations in Salt Lake City, Bountiful, Ogden, and Logan, Utah. The prophet spoke briefly and offered the

dedicatory prayer at the first session. One paragraph of the pr
eloquent prayer stands out as expressing the highest hopes
who would work and worship in this holy temple, and in other holy temples around the world: "'We seek to be like Thee,'" stated the prophet, "'we seek to pattern our lives after the life of Thy Son; we desire righteousness for ourselves and our children and our children's children. We plead with Thee to make us worthy to inherit the fulness of those blessings found only in Thy holy temples—even those blessings which grow out of a continuation of the family unit forever'" ("News of the Church," *Ensign*, March 1995, 76).

On January 12, 1995, two days before the last dedicatory session of the Bountiful Utah Temple, President Hunter was hospitalized for exhaustion. Prostate cancer had recurred and spread to his bones. The prophet remained in the hospital for four days and then returned home. For six weeks he intermittently received his counselors and others in his home as was necessary to make decisions regarding the work of the Church. On March 3, 1995, President Howard W. Hunter passed away quietly with Inis and members of the family nearby. Several days later the prophet was eulogized at fitting memorial services held in the Salt Lake Tabernacle. President Hunter's own words provide a fitting epitaph for a noble life, well lived: "Every individual person," he wrote, "has a set of challenges which sometimes seem to be earmarked for him individually. We understood that in our premortal existence. When these experiences humble, refine, and teach us, they make us better people, more grateful, loving, and considerate of other people in their own times of difficulty. Even in the most severe of times, problems and prophecies were never intended to do anything but bless the righteous and help those who are less righteous to move toward repentance" ("Why Try?" *New Era*, January 1994, 6).

SOURCES

Primary Sources

Gibbons, Francis M. Diaries, 1960–95.

Official Reports of the General Conferences of The Church of Jesus Christ of Latter-day Saints.

Books

Allen, James B. and Glen M. Leonard. *The Story of the Latter-day Saints*. 2d ed. Salt Lake City: Deseret Book, 1992.

Anderson, Joseph. *Prophets I Have Known*. Salt Lake City: Deseret Book, 1973.

Baldridge, Steven W., with Marilyn M. Rosa. *Grafting In: A History of the Latter-day Saints in the Holy Land.* Israel: The Jerusalem Branch, 1989.

Cowan, Richard O. *The Church in the Twentieth Century*. Salt Lake City: Bookcraft, 1985.

Dew, Sheri L. *Ezra Taft Benson: A Biography*. Salt Lake City: Deseret Book, 1987.

Durham, G. Homer. *N. Eldon Tanner: His Life and Service*. Salt Lake City: Deseret Book, 1986.

Encyclopedia of Mormonism. 4 vols. Edited by Daniel H. Ludlow et al. New York: Macmillan, 1992.

Gibbons, Francis M. *David O. McKay: Apostle to the World, Prophet of God*. Salt Lake City: Deseret Book, 1986.

———. *Joseph Fielding Smith: Gospel Scholar, Prophet of God*. Salt Lake City: Deseret Book, 1992.

———. *Harold B. Lee: Man of Vision, Prophet of God*. Salt Lake City: Deseret Book, 1993.

———. *Spencer W. Kimball: Resolute Disciple, Prophet of God*. Salt Lake City: Deseret Book, 1995.

———. *Ezra Taft Benson: Statesman, Patriot, Prophet of God*. Salt Lake City: Deseret Book, 1996.

Goates, L. Brent. *Harold B. Lee: Prophet and Seer*. Salt Lake City: Bookcraft, 1985.

Hill, Napoleon. *Think and Grow Rich*. New York: Fawcett Crest, 1960.

Howard, F. Burton. *Marion G. Romney: His Life and Faith*. Salt Lake City: Bookcraft, 1988.

Hymns of The Church of Jesus Christ of Latter-day Saints. Salt Lake City: The Church of Jesus Christ of Latter-day Saints, 1985.

Journal of Discourses. 26 vols. London: Latter-day Saints' Book Depot, 1854–86.

Kimball, Edward L., and Andrew E. Kimball Jr. *Spencer W. Kimball*. Salt Lake City: Bookcraft, 1977.

Knowles, Eleanor. *Howard W. Hunter*. Salt Lake City: Deseret Book, 1994.

Muir, Leo J. *A Century of Mormon Activities in California*. 2 vols. Salt Lake City: Deseret News Press, 1951–52.

O'Brien, Robert. *Hands across the Water: The Story of the Polynesian Cultural Center*. Salt Lake City: Bookcraft, 1987.

Roberts, B. H. *A Comprehensive History of The Church of Jesus Christ of Latter-day Saints, Century 1*. 6 vols. Provo, Utah: Brigham Young University Press, 1957.

Shepherd, Naomi. *Teddy Kollek: Mayor of Jerusalem*. New York: Harper and Row, 1988.

Smith, Joseph. *History of The Church of Jesus Christ of Latter-day Saints*. Edited by B. H. Roberts. 2d ed., rev. 7 vols. Salt Lake City: The Church of Jesus Christ of Latter-day Saints, 1932–51.

Tate, Lucille C. *David B. Haight: The Life Story of a Disciple*. Salt Lake City: Bookcraft, 1987.

———. *LeGrand Richards: Beloved Apostle*. Salt Lake City: Bookcraft, 1982.

Periodicals

Church News

Deseret News

Ensign

Friend

Improvement Era

New Era

Relief Society Magazine

Salt Lake Tribune

Unpublished Materials

Ferre, Craig. "A History of the Polynesian Cultural Center's Night Show, 1963–1983." Ph.D dissertation, Brigham Young University, 1988.

Hunter, Richard. "Hunter." Biography written for pamphlet introducing the Howard W. Hunter Professorship in the J. Reuben Clark Law School. Provo, Utah: Brigham Young University, 1989.

Pettit, William A. "A History of the Pasadena Stake." Manuscript, 1966.

Sorenson, John L. "Brief History of the BYU New World Archeological Foundation." Unpublished paper, April 1975.

INDEX